Dedication

This book is dedicated to all followers of Jesus who choose to put his call on their life higher than their own call.

Acknowledgements

To write a story about a young African American female pastor was probably a crazy thing to attempt as a middle-aged, non-ordained, white male. But God continues to have a sense of humor while at the same time showering me with an abundance of grace.

One of the ways God graced me was to put me in touch with several African American female pastors. Anna, Denise, Adriene, Kenita, and Jacqui, I thank each of you for sharing your insights with me, which allowed me to attempt a realistic depiction of a great leader that just happens to be a woman of color. Tim, your insights were also very helpful.

As was the case in my (our) first fable, *All Things New: A Fable of Renewal,* there is no way I could have written this story without the creativity and competence that Ann Saigeon joyfully provided. This is another story that has her fingerprints all over it and she should probably have her name on the front cover along with mine. Thank you, Ann, for your willing and skillful spirit!

I want to thank Ken, Joann, and Vicky, my close colleagues and friends, who continue to encourage me to write stories that I hope will inspire people and teach concepts that are important in the world of church revitalization and leadership.

I want to give a special note of appreciation to my friends who chose to invest in the publication of this fable by offering not only their encouragement, but also significant funds. Thank you Larry, Karen, Gord, and Rick for your belief in what this fable can do for God and for your generous blessings of all kinds!

And finally I want to thank my wife, Amanda, for her support and encouragement, the Reformed Church in America for providing me a special place to serve Christian leaders, and God, the Great I Am, who continues, bit by bit, to shape me into a follower of Christ.

Grace in the Heights:
A Fable of Revitalization

Chapter One

A Change in the Weather

BJ stood at her office window, her eyes closed, her face turned to soak in the warmth of the sun. The window was open, and she took a slow, deep breath of fresh air. It was a glorious mid-June morning. Finally the weather had warmed up and her busy life as a pastor had slowed down a little. Today she would start to catch up on tasks she had put off and maybe even get outside for a run.

BJ grabbed a stack of the previous day's mail from her desk. Sorting through ads for choir robes and appeals for donations, she came across an envelope with a handwritten address. It was from a couple at the church who had befriended her early on, when she'd first accepted the invitation to serve Grace Church. She tore it open, pulled out the single sheet of notepaper, and began to read.

> Pastor Barbara,
>
> We just can't take it anymore. Your preaching is too harsh. You are expecting us to do things that aren't reasonable, and our worship services no longer feed us.

BJ walked behind her desk and lowered herself into her chair. She shook her head slowly as she continued to read.

> We know Jesus said to love our neighbors, and even to love our enemies, but he couldn't have known the terrible

things that are done by some people who live in the neighborhood around our church.

Please don't make it so we have to leave this church or ask
you to leave. We know many others feel the same way.

We'll be paying close attention to your messages over the
next few Sundays. We just thought it was fair to let you
know that.

Charles and Deborah Pratt

BJ felt her pulse quicken. The words of a favorite author, Trisha
Taylor, came to mind: "Anxiety makes me stupid."
    "Well, something must be making *these* folks anxious, because
this note is stupid!" she heard herself say aloud.
    Barbara Jordan Thompson, "BJ" or "Pastor T" to her friends,
had served Grace Church for almost two years, first as associate
pastor and for the last ten months as the only pastor. Her call to
serve the congregation had seemed clear to her and to the members of the search committee. *But I've barely begun to lead people
in the direction of changes they absolutely have to make, and look
at what's happening already*, she thought.
    BJ grabbed her cell phone and speed dialed her mother.
Johanna picked up the call immediately.
    "Mom, I need to talk."
    "Sure, BJ." Johanna waited for BJ to continue.
    "Charles and Deborah are threatening to leave Grace. They sent
me a note saying I am asking too much of them! All I'm doing at
Grace is what they asked me to do—lead them in renewing this
congregation. Here's a couple that I thought 'got it,' and they're
saying they aren't being fed in worship anymore. They must know
we need to change things if we're going to be a welcoming place
for people who aren't eighty years old!"
    Johanna didn't jump in, and BJ continued. "They say I need to
back off or they'll leave. Or worse, they and others may try to
push me out. I'm beginning to think I shouldn't have taken this

position in the first place."

More silence. BJ was used to Johanna's way of listening. She was sure her mother was one of the wisest people ever, and she took a deep breath to calm herself as she waited for a response. Johanna finally spoke. "What do you really think, dear?"

"I think they're selfish, ignorant, and lack moral character. I can't believe Charles and Deborah, of all people, would treat me this way. They were the couple that was most influential in my decision to accept the call to come here in the first place! They were the ones more than any others who embraced me as I came on board. I can't believe they would do this, or could do this. Don't they know what this will do to a church like Grace?"

"What might be going on with them that would cause them to act this way?" Johanna asked.

BJ's voice wavered as her eyes filled with tears. "I don't know and right now I don't even care. I'm just hurt that they would do it at all."

"It's okay, baby." After a pause, Johanna continued. "Do you remember when you were sixteen and you wanted to date that boy I didn't like?

"Yes."

"And do you remember how you behaved when I said you couldn't go out with him?"

"Well, yes, I guess...but I'd rather not. Why are you asking me about that now?"

"I want to know what you think was going on in you all those years ago."

"I guess I needed to change the way I was acting, and I didn't want to." BJ was silent for a moment. "In fact, I really needed to change the way I saw the world, and that was embarrassing to have to admit. I needed to face my sinful nature, which I hated doing."

"What helped you change?"

"Well, I suppose it was the time and space you allowed for change to happen. How did you do that when I was behaving so poorly?"

"I don't know how to answer that except to say that I had faith in God and faith in you. I knew better than to try to force a six-teen-year-old to see things my way. I also knew that I couldn't give in to your anger or the bad behavior brought on by your anxiety. If I did it would lead to bigger problems down the road. I continued to do what I believed was right at the time, and I trusted in God and in you, believing that things would turn out well. I've always found God to be faithful when I've trusted. And I've always found you to come around to what is best."

"Thanks, Mom. So what do you think I should do about Charles and Deborah?"

"What do you think you should do?"

It was quiet for a few moments. When BJ spoke, Johanna sensed that she had left some of her anxiety behind.

"I could continue to do what I think is best…not get too tangled up in my anger toward them…let them deal with their issues themselves and with God." She paused. "I could give them grace…and space to grow on their own terms. I could have faith that God will guide them over the coming years. I could offer them, at least in my heart, a prayer of blessing if they do choose to leave Grace—even if they go out spitting nails at me!"

"That's quite an image," said Johanna, laughing. BJ laughed a little too.

"Amazing! Where does a young woman like you get all this wisdom?"

Johanna started to pray, as she sometimes did after she and BJ had a deep conversation. "Lord, thank you for the amazing gift that is my daughter. I am so privileged that you entrusted her to me. It's easy to see the big things you have before her. Help me to love her in ways that give her strength, courage, and clarity of vision. Lord, we love you, and we want to do whatever you ask of us."

BJ broke in. "Jesus, thank you for my mother, for her love, encouragement, and wisdom. Help me lead well in the challenging and worthy journey I'm on with you. Move in the hearts of the people you are calling to make Grace a place that is pleasing to you and that brings glory to your name. Help us fight our fear of the unknown. Help us let go of the needs of our egos and others' hurtful behaviors. Remind us that you are always there with us when we are ready to seek you at deeper levels. Jesus, help us to seek you in deeper ways, especially when our darkened eyes are missing your light. Thank you, Lord. It's in your holy name we pray. Amen!

"Thanks, Mom, I feel much better. I'll call again soon, but right now I think I need to get in touch with Charles and Deborah."

* * * * *

Johanna had been expecting this call from BJ. She had known from the beginning how difficult her daughter's new ministry would be. She also knew strong leaders like BJ often experienced intense anger and even hatred from some of their followers as the changes those leaders drove started to take place...even changes that the followers themselves had requested.

Moving into an uncertain future and the anxiety it produces can do that to people, thought Johanna. People seldom understand that the changes they most desire will force them to make much deeper changes than they had imagined. At some point, many will start to react strongly against the changes.

Johanna had recognized her daughter's gifts for leadership from an early age, and she had been preparing Barbara for the kind of role she had now for more than twenty years. Johanna herself valued strong leadership so much that she had named her daughter after Barbara Jordan. Jordan, a civil rights leader, was the first African American elected to the Texas Senate after the Reconstruction era, and the first black woman from a southern state ever elected to the U.S. House of Representatives.

In various circumstances, Johanna had often told BJ that if she, Johanna, had understood what would be required of her when she chose to do one thing or another, she never would have agreed to do it. Then she would always add, "But I am so thankful I didn't understand, because now I love the fact that I did it!" Now it was BJ's turn to experience that life lesson firsthand.

Johanna smiled as she thought about how stubborn BJ could be; it was a trait she'd inherited from her mom. Once BJ had set her mind to doing something good and worthwhile, she was sure to finish the journey. She wouldn't even see that there was a choice in the matter.

Johanna knew BJ would need to be stubborn to bring change to Grace Church. Over many generations, members there had gradually developed treasured traditions, personal preferences, and rooted relationships, and put each ahead of God's call on their lives. Anyone who messed with "the way it has always been done" risked being attacked by "religious antibodies" and expelled like a foreign substance.

Fundamentally changing an organization guaranteed days like the one BJ was having this particular Monday. Johanna knew she'd be most helpful by being ready to listen. That was the best way she knew to love her daughter at a time like this.

Chapter Two

Grace on a Journey

The journey of renewal that BJ had been called to lead at Grace Church began with events that had taken place several years before she had come on board.

Back then the previous long-time pastor of Grace, Pastor Henry, and a large number of members had engaged in a deeply spiritual and intense season of discernment regarding the future of Grace Church.

They had undertaken this season of discernment thanks to the leadership of Bob Withey, a support pastor supplied by the group of ministers and elders who had oversight of the church district where Grace Church was located. Bob helped the people of Grace Church come to realize that if their ministry in Jefferson Heights was going to live on, they needed to make big changes.

The average age of members was sixty-four, long-time members were dying off, and attendance was just a fraction of what it had been in the church's glory days. No one who attended lived within five miles of the church, and it was doubtful that anyone in the neighborhood would care, or even notice, if Grace Church closed its doors.

The season of discernment was kicked off by a weekend retreat. During the retreat church leaders revisited the congregation's mission and values. They also clarified their vision with regard to where God was calling them to join with what God was already doing and wanted to do in Jefferson Heights.

As the leaders went through this discernment process together, they realized that to lead them into ministry in an ever changing world, and especially in their changed neighborhood, they needed a new pastoral leader. Pastor Henry had started planning for retirement, and they decided to look for an associate pastor who could one day lead them toward the new future they had

begun to envision—a future that would involve welcoming and
worshiping with people from the church's neighborhood.

They realized that they needed to begin by becoming more
open and by inviting people in the surrounding community to
come to Grace Church. Their goal was that over the next ten years
the church would become a welcoming place for people of all
races and all ages.

The leaders spent months reading about and researching cross-
cultural ministry. They attended weekend seminars on the topic,
and invited anyone from the congregation who was interested to
come along. Only a few folks signed up, which was discouraging,
but not half as discouraging as what they learned through their
reading and seminars: Grace Church's road of transition from an
all-white congregation to one that embraced its community was
going to be very difficult if it succeeded at all.

Pastor Henry and the elders introduced the vision and goal to
the congregation in a series of sermons and after-service discussions. They learned that while most of Grace Church's members
said they believed that all people, "red, yellow, black, and white,"
are precious in God's sight, they had no idea how huge the racial,
social, cultural, and economic barriers were that stood between
them and the people from different backgrounds who lived and
worked near the church. It was becoming clear how difficult it
was going to be for Grace Church to become involved in the community and to become a welcoming congregation for the people
who lived nearby.

When Grace Church put the word out that they were looking
for an associate pastor who would eventually become lead pastor,
only three people responded. Two were in their late fifties and
seemed more interested in finding a job than pursuing a call from
God. But the response from the third person, Barbara Jordan
Thompson, convinced members of the search committee that she
was eager to take on the challenge of connecting Grace and its
neighbors.

Once they realized that Barbara was African American the committee members had a few interesting, and sometimes difficult,
discussions. Would the older members of this all-white congrega-

tion respect the leadership of someone who was black, female, and single? Would Barbara feel at home leading such a congregation? Would she want to hang in there long enough to follow through with the changes that needed to happen?

After a lot of deliberation and prayer they came to believe that calling a pastor of color was probably just what was needed. With equal amounts of excitement and anxiety, Grace Church called Barbara Thompson.

BJ had accepted the call with the understanding that she would become the solo pastor in a few years, and it happened more quickly than she had expected. Just a year after she arrived, Henry retired. It was more responsibility than BJ had expected so soon, but she was excited to be given a chance to lead a church. Grace Church would become the multiracial, multicultural church that God had given her a vision for all those years ago.

It would be a church that was committed to Christ and his teachings. A church that was selfless, just like Christ. It would be a church blessed beyond imagination because of God's love. A church filled with people who would reach out to the lost and broken and whose members would experience greater abundance of life than they had ever thought possible. The same abundant life that the apostle Paul received on his way to Damascus. The abundant life that led Paul to live knowing he had something wonderful deep inside that others couldn't touch no matter how they treated him. It was an abundance that went beyond anything earthly.

BJ was ready to lead like Paul and thrilled to show others what it meant to live the abundant life and invite them to join in.

Chapter Three

The Power of Listening

BJ sat down at her desk and read the Pratts' letter one more time. She would put her other tasks aside and call to set up a meeting with Charles and Deborah right away.

Before making the call, she reviewed a conflict-resolution model that Johanna had introduced her to years ago, before she had enrolled in seminary in answer to God's call to ministry. Back then BJ worked as a junior account executive with a high-powered ad agency that had recruited her straight out of college. The conflict-resolution model, called "Leaning into Healthy Conflict," had helped her resolve issues with several people at the agency. Each time, following the model had also helped strengthen her relationship with the other person.

Now that she was a pastor, however, the dynamics felt different. There wasn't really any room for negotiation, because BJ had such a clear vision of what needed to happen at Grace Church. It was going to be hard for her to see things from the Pratts' perspective. She needed to understand why they felt the way they did, but she wasn't willing to compromise when it came to staying faithful to God's leading for Grace Church. She would do the right thing even if it was the hard thing. As Johanna had often said, "It isn't about doing what's easy. It's about doing what's best."

BJ picked up her phone to call the Pratts, and then paused. She thought she heard footsteps outside her office, from somewhere down the hall. BJ walked to her office door and peered into the dim hallway just in time to see someone slip into the church library.

BJ called, "Hello?" She walked down the hall, toward the front door of the church, and stopped just outside the open door to the library. The library blinds were closed, and in the darkened room she could just make out the silhouette of a young woman standing near a bookcase. BJ reached for the switch just inside the doorway and flipped on the lights.

"How can I help you?" asked BJ.

The woman, who appeared to be about seventeen or eighteen years old, just stared at BJ. For a few seconds she seemed to contemplate making a run for it. Then she sighed. "I just need a place to hang out for a little while. My boyfriend's...looking for me."

"I'm BJ Thompson." BJ walked toward the young woman and held out her hand. "Folks call me Pastor T."

"I'm Trina." Trina clasped BJ's hand briefly and then started to step away.

"Trina, you're welcome to stay. Let's walk back to my office where we can talk."

Trina followed her. BJ sat in one of two overstuffed chairs in a corner of her office and motioned for Trina to take the other.

Trina sat straight up in the chair and looked down at her hands, which she held tightly together. "This seemed like a good place to hide." A brief, conflicted smile crossed her face. "No one would expect to find me in a church!" She looked up. "I'm sorry to bother you."

"You're not a bother. Can you tell me why you're hiding from your friend?"

Trina twisted her hands and glanced out the window. "Well, he's okay most of the time, and then sometimes he gets so mad. I knew I was going to get...yelled at."

BJ didn't push. She thought she had seen Trina before, hanging out in the park just down the street. She wore black high-heeled boots, a short, black spandex skirt, and a low-cut silky shirt printed with big red flowers. Huge neon-pink earrings and assorted gold rings and studs completed her ensemble.

BJ also noticed big bruises on Trina's arms and legs. The thought flashed through her mind that Trina's boyfriend might really be her pimp.

BJ kept the conversation light. She learned that Trina had grown up just a few blocks away, and she had once dreamed of owning her own designer clothing store. Instead she had to drop out of school in tenth grade to take care of her younger brother when her mom died of cancer.

BJ was thinking how neat it was that this young woman had stayed to talk when Trina glanced at BJ's desk clock and jumped out of her chair. "Oh my god—oops, sorry Pastor T—it's late! I gotta go!" Trina sprinted into the hall and out the door in a flash. BJ was amazed to see how fast she could move in those heels.

BJ watched from her office window as Trina half-walked, half-ran down the sidewalk to meet a woman who looked quite a bit older. They started laughing and pushing each other playfully. BJ continued to watch and saw Trina glance back at the church before she and her friend headed toward the small park down the street.

She paused and listened in case God would speak to her heart, give her some sense of what her meeting with Trina was all about, but nothing came to mind. Still, BJ sensed that she and Trina would meet again. She would just have to wait to see how it would come about.

Her morning run would have to wait too. It was time to make that phone call and set up a time to talk with Deborah and Charles. She would have to fit it in before the hospital visits she planned to make to two ailing members of the church.

* * * * *

"Charles, this is Pastor Barbara."

"Oh, hi, Pastor."

"I received the note you and Deborah sent me, and I want to get together with the two of you to talk. Do you have time in the next day or so?

Charles sounded flustered. "Well, ah…let me check with Deborah. She's not home right now. Can I call you back?"

"Sure. I look forward to learning more about the perspective you shared in your note."

"Uh, okay. Call you later. Bye."

BJ didn't think she would get a call back. She typed a reminder in her calendar to call Charles again in two days.

Chapter Four

The Power of Understanding

It was Tuesday. BJ was usually disciplined about dedicating Tuesday morning to prayer and spiritual retreat, followed by an afternoon of study and preparation for Sunday's message. She had made a pre-surgery visit at six that morning with one of Grace's widows, and now she sat in one of the comfy chairs in her office to pray, still hoping to get a call from Charles or Deborah. She couldn't help wondering why one or the other hadn't yet called her. Didn't people feel ashamed when they chickened out?

She also found herself praying for Trina and decided to take a quick walk around the block to see if she could spot her. BJ trotted down the front steps of Grace Church, and set out toward the park. She walked around and across the park grounds, but she didn't see Trina anywhere. Back at church again she prayed, "Lord, please be with Trina and protect her from any forces that would hurt her. Help me know how to love her...and also how to love Charles and Deborah."

BJ settled in for more prayer and study. She pulled her iPod out of her handbag and listened to her favorite inspirational music as she prayed for a list of people that included some she loved and some she was still learning to love. She prayed for the Heights neighborhood, and again for Trina. She asked God for clarity and courage to lead the group of Christians who gathered at Grace Church to go where God was calling them to go and to become what God had created them to be.

By noon, BJ felt renewed and clear headed. She left her office by its side door, crossing the parking lot to the parsonage for a quick lunch. Then she returned to her office to engage the scripture passage that would be the foundation for her message that Sunday: Matthew 7:1-5.

> Do not judge, so that you may not be judged. For with the
> judgment you make you will be judged, and the measure
> you give will be the measure you get. Why do you see the
> speck in your neighbor's eye, but do not notice the log in
> your own eye? Or how can you say to your neighbor, "Let
> me take the speck out of your eye," while the log is in your
> own eye? You hypocrite, first take the log out of your own
> eye, and then you will see clearly to take the speck out of
> your neighbor's eye.

As was often the case, the passage spoke directly to her about
things she was dealing with herself. Not judging Trina and how
she was living her life was relatively easy for BJ. Not judging
Charles and Deborah was a bigger challenge.

"Ours is not to judge," she said out loud. Questions popped up
in her mind. *Why are we not to judge? Is it just so others don't become overloaded with guilt due to our judgment, or did God give
us that instruction for our own good? Does not judging others
make us more joyful or more holy? If it does, then why does it feel
so good to judge? Hmm...I wonder what log might be in my eye?
What logs might be in the eyes of people in our congregation?*

She continued to reflect on the verse, on judging others, and on
the problem of hypocrisy. *I wonder if judging others somehow
makes me feel like the judgment spotlight is off me? What happens
when I ignore the log in my own eye? Does it just make me feel better or are there other consequences?*

Reflecting on these questions helped her deal with her feelings
toward Charles and Deborah. It also reminded her that, but for the
grace of God, she could be in their shoes right now.

BJ smiled. God was building her trust by giving her just what
she needed at the very moment she needed it.

After a few hours of study, research, reflection, and writing, BJ
felt a powerful peace come over her. She went into the restroom
just outside her office and changed into her running clothes. She
couldn't resist going back to her office to glance at her email just

for a moment. So of course it was another thirty minutes before she dragged herself away and bounded out the church doors for a three-mile run.

As she ran BJ thought about how much exercise meant to her. She remembered a parable her mom had told her about the importance of getting the big rocks in your jar before allowing the pebbles and sand to fill it up. It was about making sure to give priority to the things that were really important to leading a full life. For BJ those things were prayer, getting into the Scriptures, and running. If she let her jar—her life—fill up with everything else that wanted to come in, there would be no way to get the stuff in that was most critical for her, the big rocks. All the sand and pebbles would prevent that.

For BJ, Tuesday was the day of the week that she made sure to put in the big rocks before all of the other urgent and important pebbles filled her jar. She had gotten in productive prayer and study time and a good run—it had been a great day so far. BJ hopped into her car and drove to Jefferson City Hospital to check on the Grace member who had undergone surgery earlier in the day.

That evening, while she was catching up on phone calls, BJ got a call from Johanna, who wanted to find out how she was doing. They talked for an hour, but this time it was mostly catching up on what Johanna had been doing. Johanna was an active leader in the community where she lived, and faced her own set of challenges. Over the past couple of days Johanna had been composing a pointed letter to send to the local paper's editorial department. It was about the need to find better ways to encourage young people to stay in high school until they graduated. BJ felt good being a listener for Johanna this time, and she had a chance to tell her about Trina and the hard turn the young woman's life had taken after she'd had to drop out of school.

* * * * *

On Wednesday morning, BJ kept to her Wednesday-through-Saturday discipline of about a half-hour of Bible reading and prayer. She glanced through the local paper over breakfast, and then headed across the strip of grass between the parsonage and her office for another busy day. It was nine o'clock, and she decided to call Charles right off the bat.

"Hi, Charles, this is Pastor Barbara. How are you today?"

"Hi, Barbara. I'm fine. You?" Charles sounded surprised to hear from her.

"I'm fine on this beautiful morning. Thank you for asking. I'm hoping we can get together today or tomorrow."

"Well, I forgot to ask Deborah when she might be able to join us, so we should wait till I check with her. I can call you in a couple of days."

BJ decided to push past what might have been a stalling tactic. "Well, I would really like to meet today or tomorrow. Could we set up a time that works for you and me, hoping that Deborah can join us?"

Her assertiveness seemed to throw Charles off balance, maybe especially because she sounded so friendly. Words seem to fly out of his mouth in spite of himself. "Sure, what about lunch today?"

"Great. Let's meet at Ally's Place at noon. I'll buy."

Charles paused. BJ thought he was going to back out, but he simply said, "See you then."

BJ had learned years ago at a Boys and Girls Club, first as a member and later as a young volunteer, that leadership is influence. She had learned how to get kids to do good deeds that they wouldn't otherwise have done. Through relationship skills and appealing to their sense of right and wrong, she could get kids to change their behavior. She could influence them to do things they might not like to do, but that they knew they should do. One of her favorite quotes, the words of former Dallas Cowboys coach Tom Landry, had been posted on the wall at the club: "My job is to get players to do things they don't want to do to become the players they want to be."

She knew she would need to adopt that mentality with lots of the members of Grace, including Charles. He had been one of the most outspoken supporters of the vision to connect Grace with its neighborhood, and he had said yes to meeting her for lunch, but he clearly did not want to have a conversation.

* * * * *

After a morning of phone calls, visits, and emails BJ quickly walked the three blocks past storefronts and apartment buildings to Ally's Place. Dark clouds were moving in overhead. If it started to rain, BJ thought, she would have to ask Charles for a ride back to church. She smiled. Johanna had taught her long ago that if you want to make a new friend, offer to do them a favor, but if you want to make a really good friend, ask them to do you a favor.

She arrived five minutes before noon. Charles wasn't there yet, and Ally greeted her with a big, "Hi there, how you doing, Pastor T?"

"I'm great, Ally, thanks for asking." BJ thought Ally was a stitch—feisty and fun. And she treated everyone the same, from the mayor to the trash collector. Everyone in the Heights seemed to know Ally, and her home-style cooking was hard to beat.

"Meeting anyone special?" Ally asked, giving BJ a wink. BJ knew Ally was hoping it was Michael, the man BJ had been dating for over a year. Michael and Ally always had fun trading stories and shooting the breeze.

"I wish it was Michael, Ally. No, he's out of town for a few more days. I'm meeting a member of our congregation, Charles Pratt, and maybe his wife."

"Well, sit right over here. You can watch the storm." Ally led the way to a forties-era Formica-topped table that had one end pulled up to the big front window. A few raindrops spotted the sidewalk just beyond the plate glass.

BJ sighed. There might be more than one kind of storm on the way. She jumped as lightning flashed and a loud crack of thunder boomed. A few more customers arrived, but it seemed like the weather was keeping most of the regulars away. If Charles didn't show, BJ thought, she might have no way back to the church for a while.

Ally returned with water and a menu. "You know this menu by heart, but your friend might need one." Ally walked back to the lunch counter and started refilling rows of salt shakers and ketchup bottles.

BJ spotted Charles across the street. He looked side to side before dashing over to the restaurant. She mentally went over the first steps of the conflict resolution model she planned to use: state your observation or perspective within thirty seconds; then do one thing, and one thing only—seek to understand the other person's perspective regarding your observation.

Charles spotted BJ as he pushed through the door. "Hi, Pastor. Deborah couldn't come. Some storm, huh?"

BJ let the awkward pause that followed hang in the air. Charles took a seat across the table from her. "Thanks for meeting me today, Charles. Do you need time to look at the menu?"

"No, I eat here once in a while. I'm all set."

BJ jumped right in. "Charles, I was surprised to receive your note Monday morning. I was disappointed that you didn't come to talk with me face to face. I need to understand more of what's behind what you wrote. Please help me understand more deeply what is bothering you."

"Well, we are...," he paused and took a deep breath; he seemed to be collecting his thoughts. BJ could sense his emotions starting to rise as he continued. "We're angry that you have chosen to create your own vision for our future when we called you to Grace Church to do something else."

BJ was confused. Hadn't she been doing exactly what the search team had called her to do? But she had learned to listen in order to fully understand another person's perceptions before seeking to be understood by that person.

"Charles, please tell me what you understand I was called to do at Grace."

"Sure I will." BJ thought she heard a bit of an edge to his tone.

Just then Ally walked up. "What would y'all like?" Ally was frowning, all business, none of her usual kidding around, and BJ thought she must have picked up on the tension between her and Charles.

They ordered and Charles continued. "We called you here to help us bring the community into our church, so that they would experience us and feel what a loving place it is and how meaningful our worship is. We called you to help us reach out to them...so that they would hear the good news. I thought you understood that our future depends on growing our congregation, and that we feel we need to do that with people in the immediate community. We were very clear about this during the interviews."

BJ responded with a fervent "Amen!" and then asked, "How does what I am doing fail to meet those expectations?"

"Isn't it obvious? We thought you would be out in the community telling people about us. You know, with what you learned in your professional background, sort of marketing us so people would start to come to our services."

BJ just stared at Charles, and he pushed ahead. "We need you to attract people to Grace so they can get their lives on the right path. We are ready and willing to help these people find God, and get to know and follow God. But you seem to be spending more time preaching to us about how we need to change! It's like you think we're the bad guys here!"

His voice had gotten louder, and he glanced over toward Ally, who stood at the lunch counter rewriting a chalkboard menu. Then Charles sat back and looked at BJ with narrowed eyes. "What do you have to say about this?"

"Charles, I can see your perspective now, and I couldn't previously. Thank you for your willingness to share it even though it was probably uncomfortable for you."

Her gracious response was not what Charles had expected. His voice was quieter as he said, "I'm curious. What did you think we were asking you to do?"

"Well, in large part we see the same end goal. We want Grace to be a place where the community will visit, come to know the love of Christ, become a part of us, and be loved and nurtured in their faith." Charles nodded in agreement.

BJ continued. "However, I think we view how to pursue that goal in very different ways. My sense is that we need to go into the community and engage our neighbors as Jesus would. That we need to get to know them, serve them, love them in ways they can appreciate and understand. Then, and only then, they might be willing to overcome the barriers that keep them from walking through our doors in the first place."

Charles stiffened. "What do you mean by 'barriers that keep them from walking through our doors in the first place'?"

BJ prayed inwardly for the right words to say to Charles. "Many of our neighbors have been mistreated by people who look just like you," she began, "and like Deborah and everyone else in our congregation. They don't necessarily think all white people are bad or would mistreat them. But many really don't trust people who look like you. They can't see your heart. They can't see your desire to help them, to love them. They have virtually no interaction with us. Our folks drive into the parking lot and walk into the church, and then a little while later they jump back in their cars and drive away to the suburbs."

Charles was still listening, so she pushed ahead. "If they did start to interact with our members in some way, their past experience would likely lead them to believe you'd only want to 'fix' them, to help them become just like you, which is a way of saying they aren't viewed by white people as equal human beings, equally and fully loved by God without regard to their race or income or social status.

"Also, some of our neighbors have never been in a church that looks like ours—one with bricks and columns and beautiful stained glass windows. To them it might look formidable, intimidating, like an ivy covered hall on Harvard's campus. To many, I'm sure it looks institutional, like a school or a hospital. And many of our neighbors have been mistreated by the institutions they have come in contact with."

BJ was encouraged to see Charles's expression soften. "If they did come inside, what do you expect they would experience?" she continued. "Loving people who would come up and give them a warm handshake and friendly eye contact? Or people staying at arm's length and casting distrusting and judgmental glances?

"Charles, the best marketing in the world won't open the doors of Grace Church for the people of Jefferson Heights. The only thing that will draw people to Grace is the love of Jesus. And the way they'll experience that love is through people like you." She paused, waiting for Charles to respond.

"It's something to think about for sure," he said. BJ was gratified that it sounded like he really meant it.

Lightning flashed and a deep roll of thunder shook the window.

Rain fell like it was being poured from a watering can. BJ turned to Charles. "Could I ask you for a favor?"

"Of course."

"Would you give me a ride back to the church, by way of Hunter Park? I walked here and I'll have a really bad hair day if I have to walk back. I also want to see if I can spot a woman who stopped at the church earlier this week. She seems to hang around the park a lot."

"No problem. Glad to."

They finished their lunch and Charles left to get his car as BJ took care of the bill. Ally gave her another little wink. "You be careful. This storm could go on for a while."

In more ways than you know, sister, in more ways than you know, BJ thought as she smiled and winked back at Ally. She said, "I appreciate your concern, Ally. Say a prayer for me."

BJ pushed open the door, ran a few steps through the pouring rain, and slipped into the front passenger seat of Charles's car.

Chapter Five

When Worlds Collide

They passed the church and rode alongside Hunter Park. Just ahead, BJ spotted Trina standing in the park's bus-stop shelter. "Charles, would you pull over near that woman in the red jacket?"

He pulled up to the curb in front of the bus stop. BJ stepped out of the car and joined Trina under the shelter.

"Trina! This is some storm, isn't it?"

Trina stared up the street, away from BJ, and mumbled. "Hi, Pastor. I didn't recognize you right away."

BJ could barely hear her above the racket of rain on the bus stop's Plexiglas roof. "Are you waiting for the bus? Can we give you a ride somewhere?"

Trina turned and BJ noticed a fresh bruise below her right eye. "No. I mean, I'm just trying to stay dry." Her words came out slow and flat.

"Well, it's a short drive to the church. If you're not busy this afternoon, would you be willing to help with a small project I have going?"

Trina hesitated, then shrugged. "Okay. I could help for a little while I guess." Trina got into the backseat of Charles's car. She and Charles muttered tentative hi's.

"Trina's going to help me in the church library, Charles, so you can just drop us both off at Grace." He shot her a look full of misgiving.

A couple of minutes later, Charles pulled to the curb in front of Grace Church. He glanced at Trina in the rearview mirror then over at BJ. "I can come in if you like." Trina rolled her eyes. She made a quick exit from Charles's car, bounded up the church steps, and turned to wait for BJ.

"No thanks, Charles. I'm looking forward to catching up with Trina…just us girls."

Trina smiled as BJ joined her in front of the church door. "Thanks, Pastor T."

BJ watched Charles drive slowly away. He looked back a couple of times before disappearing in traffic. BJ just waved. She held open the heavy wooden church door for Trina and followed her in.

"So, Trina, tell me how you're doing." Trina took off her jacket. BJ couldn't help noticing more fresh bruises on her arms in addition to the one under her eye.

"Oh, okay." Noticing the questioning expression in BJ's eyes, she added, "I fell yesterday, but it wasn't too bad."

BJ and Trina spent the next few hours fixing up a corner of the library just for kids, stopping only to go downstairs to the kitchen to find something for Trina to nibble on. They sorted through boxes of children's books that a Grace member had donated recently. Of course, there weren't any kids attending Grace yet, but BJ saw the new kids' corner as a step of faith. It was one more way to say things were going to change.

Trina and BJ brushed bright acrylic paints on the library walls, filling in the outline of a big Noah's Ark and pairs of animals that an artist who attended the church had sketched at BJ's request. Then Trina painted a sun and BJ added a rainbow.

"Trina, we make a good team," said BJ, standing back to admire their handiwork. "We just need a few kid-sized tables and chairs, and it'll be perfect!"

They talked the whole time they worked together, and a few of Trina's comments made BJ realize that she knew the Noah's Ark story. BJ was curious. She wondered if Trina had once attended church or a children's program. Or maybe her mom or grandmother had read her the story when she was little.

BJ didn't press for details. Trina showed signs of being uncomfortable whenever the conversation focused on her. She didn't want to talk about her living arrangements, her boyfriend, or much of anything else to do with her personal life. BJ did discover that they shared a love of music and that Trina was familiar with some of BJ's favorite inspirational artists. Trina, for her part, was curious about BJ's path to being a pastor, a story BJ was happy to share.

As BJ and Trina cleaned up and put away the paints and brushes, they could see through the library window that the sun shone brightly even though rain continued to fall. "There must be a real rainbow somewhere out there today," said BJ. "These are the perfect conditions for one. They're hard to see in the city, though, with all the buildings in the way."

"I'd better get going," said Trina.

BJ walked Trina to the church doors, hesitated, and then asked, "Trina, can I say a short prayer before you go?"

Trina looked uncomfortable, but she didn't refuse. "Sure. It's what preachers do, right?"

BJ asked God to bless Trina and their new friendship. She also asked that both she and Trina would be kept safe. She gave Trina a quick hug. "Listen, I can put you in touch with a women's shelter if you need that. And you can call me anytime."

"Thanks, Pastor T." Trina's voice was husky, and BJ thought she might start to cry. Trina quickly turned away and slipped through the church doors. BJ stepped outside too. She took a deep breath of rain scented air as she watched Trina head toward the park. Trina turned to wave a couple of times. The clouds were breaking up and a light breeze shook water from the scrawny tree planted between the sidewalk and the street. BJ felt hopeful and enormously tired at the same time.

When she returned to her office desk, it was almost five o'clock. She was getting ready to return more calls and emails before heading home when Deborah phoned.

"Pastor T, Charles told me all about your talk at lunch today. I know he's sorry about the note we sent you. I am too. Please forgive me. We've been frustrated, but we should have come to talk to you in person. Anyway, I hope you'll forgive us."

"Of course, Deborah. I do forgive you. But I also have to tell you, there's one part of your note I really hope you follow through on."

Deborah seemed to hold her breath. "Really?"

"Yes," said BJ, smiling. "The part where you promise to pay especially close attention to my messages over the next few Sundays.

I hope you do!"

"Oh!" Deborah sounded relieved and gave a little laugh. "Thanks so much, Pastor T. I look forward to it."

As soon as they'd hung up, BJ called Johanna. Her voicemail picked up and BJ left a message.

> Mom, I hope you've had a good day. I just wanted to let you know I had great conversations with Charles and Deborah. Thanks again for your counsel and encouragement. Give me a call when you get a chance. Love you.

* * * * *

Thanks in part to her experience with Deborah and Charles, BJ's preaching that Sunday made Matthew 7:1-5 come alive. She spoke passionately about the crucial role of reconciliation in building a multiracial congregation.

As BJ drew her sermon to a close, she asked, "So what do we do? What has God been leading us toward?

"First of all, we must recognize that we need to change our attitudes before we'll be able to reach our neighbors. All of us are lost and broken without God. We have learned of God's good news, and that God has given us a road to redemption. The only real difference between those of us who are inside the walls of Grace and those who are on the outside is that we know the good news. If we think we are ultimately different in God's eyes—maybe better or somehow more deserving than the people outside our walls—then we have lost the struggle before we have even begun.

"We have to remind ourselves that people who find themselves in tough situations didn't necessarily choose to be in them. 'But for the grace of God, there go I.' I believe we need to go to them, like Jesus did, to love them, listen to them, learn from them, understand their world as best we can, engage their world. Like most people, deep down they are thinking, 'I don't care how much you know until I know how much you care.'

"Once we have built relationships of love and trust with people, then, and only then, can we challenge people to come to know Jesus and pursue living a holy life. And we must recognize that we are challenged to live holy lives as well.

"I'm sorry that I didn't fully understand the perspective of many people in this congregation. Some of you were hoping that just having me as pastor would somehow express to our neighbors that Grace was a welcoming community. I hope you now see that I have been doing what I believe God has called me to do. I am called to lead the people of God's church, Grace Church, to learn a new way to love our neighbors. I hope you can see that I have been doing what I believe you called me here to do. Grace has no future unless we become relevant in this community. Otherwise we might as well call in hospice and figure out how to die with dignity.

"People, there is inside-the-walls work to be done at Grace Church. It will be some of the hardest work you've ever done. But I believe strongly that it will be some of the most rewarding work you have ever done as well."

BJ led the congregation in a prayer of rededication to embrace the changes God wanted to lead them through. It was going to take a lot of changes to build a bridge of understanding and care to people in the neighborhood around Grace Church. She was encouraged that most folks stayed after the service for coffee and conversation. The mood seemed upbeat in spite of the hard message she'd delivered.

After most of the people had left, Charles walked up to BJ.

"Barbara, I'm sorry about the way I reacted. I think I understand now how you're going about giving us a chance to become a church that people in this neighborhood will feel welcome at. If I feel the need to sound off about something in the future, I'll do it face to face."

"That means a lot to me, Charles. Thank you. I believe God is glad we're working together again, and God is going to do some wonderful things through both of us. I also believe that the people who are now inside the walls of Grace will be every bit as blessed as those who will find their way here in the months and years to come."

* * * * *

Leaving church after the service, BJ spotted Michael waiting for her in his car in the church parking lot. He was a member at a church a few miles away and had yet to attend a service at Grace. He'd returned from his trip just a few days ago, and he and BJ were finally going to get a chance to catch up.

Michael and BJ had talked daily by phone over the past week. BJ had heard all about the continuing education class Michael had been attending. He needed the class to keep his accreditation as a science teacher at a Jefferson City middle school. Michael had heard the highlights of BJ's conversations with the Pratts, although she hadn't referred to them by name. He had also heard quite a bit about Trina.

He watched as BJ said good-bye to one last person and turned to walk to his car. He hopped out from behind the wheel to give her a quick hug and a kiss. "How about a nice dinner and a long conversation?" Michael walked around the car and opened the passenger door for BJ.

"Sounds divine!" BJ hopped in.

He leaned in through the car window. "I made a big pot of gumbo, lots of shrimp."

"Michael, you know the way to my heart! I'm so hungry I could eat the whole pot."

"Well, too bad, you have to share." Michael grinned. He walked back to the driver's side of the car, slipped behind the wheel, and pulled her close. "Good to see you, babe."

"Michael, I'm so glad you're back."

She started telling him about her message that morning. "It probably was tough for people to hear," she said, "but I thought they received it pretty well."

"That's good to hear. Let's hit the road, and you can tell me more about it." He closed the car windows and flipped on the air conditioning. Under cloudless skies, the temperature was rising fast.

After stuffing themselves on gumbo and rice at Michael's place, they decided to drive to a nearby town to visit Luann and Rob. Michael had become close friends with the young couple in college, and they'd recently married and bought a house. Michael called ahead to find out if it would be okay if he and BJ dropped by. Rob told Michael sure, if they were prepared to veg by the pool. Michael said he was pretty sure that wasn't going to be a problem.

Chapter Six

Preach It!
Live It!

S pending Sunday afternoon catching up with Luann and Rob
and relaxing around their pool had been like therapy. BJ's
calm carried over into her Tuesday morning spiritual retreat
time. Her afternoon study brought an encounter with a scripture
passage that spoke deeply to her—John 21:15-17.

> When they had finished breakfast, Jesus said to Simon
> Peter, "Simon son of John, do you love me more than
> these?" He said to him, "Yes, Lord; you know that I love
> you." Jesus said to him, "Feed my lambs." A second time
> he said to him, "Simon son of John, do you love me?" He
> said to him, "Yes, Lord; you know that I love you." Jesus
> said to him, "Tend my sheep." He said to him the third
> time, "Simon son of John, do you love me?" Peter felt hurt
> because he said to him the third time, "Do you love me?"
> And he said to him, "Lord, you know everything; you
> know that I love you." Jesus said to him, "Feed my sheep."

BJ read the passage half a dozen times, memorizing it and letting the words wash over her. She sensed God calling her to lead
her flock. She read commentaries on the passage and paused to ask
the Holy Spirit to help her understand what to focus on and share
with the congregation.

BJ closed her eyes and listened for God's still, small voice. She
tried to eliminate the noise in her head and clear space for ideas
that might not be hers. The words "feed my sheep" kept coming to
mind. A simple phrase. So basic and yet packed with so much
meaning.

It drew her into deeper reflection on what it means to truly love
Jesus. What did it mean for her to see others as children of God?
Why had she been blessed with being born to Johanna? She had
been deeply loved and nurtured as a child. Why had she been
given such clarity about what a church could and should be for
Christ?

"Feed my sheep." The words seemed to resonate deep within
her. What did it mean to feed Jesus' sheep? Did it mean to feed the
members of Grace? Or did it mean to feed the lost and broken people living in the Heights?

BJ drifted back in memory to a time when she thought all people were blessed like she was. When she was a child, she had assumed that everyone had a great parent or two. She had learned
over time that many didn't. It became clear that she had been
richly blessed by being born to Johanna, who helped her discover
that she had gifts that could only have come from God. Amazing
experiences in school, at church, and as a volunteer had helped
her develop those gifts. And the greatest gift of all had been to be
drawn by God to faith in God. She had come to believe that her
faith was a gift from God, and she knew that God's hand had always been leading her to this place.

She felt overwhelmed with God's grace and with sadness for
those who had not received these same kinds of blessings. She
didn't understand why God would bless her so richly and apparently not bless others.

"Feed my sheep."

She saw clearly that Grace was a congregation filled with people
to whom much had been given, and that over the years they had
made little effort to share those blessings with their neighbors in
the Heights. She saw how important it would be for her to help
people understand what she was seeing, what she was feeling,
what she was convinced God wanted them to understand. Luke
12:48 came to mind: "From everyone to whom much has been
given, much will be required; and from the one to whom much has
been entrusted, even more will be demanded."

Once again she felt convicted about the vision for Grace Church
becoming a welcoming congregation. It could be summed up by

the command Jesus gave to Peter. It was the rock that the church was built on—"feed my sheep."

It was becoming clear: she was to feed both the members of Grace and the people of the Heights. And one of the most important ways to spiritually feed the members of Grace would be to help them experience the abundant life promised to those who are willing to die to self in order to follow God's mission in the world. That mission was captured for BJ by three simple words: feed my sheep.

It was clear that she needed to help members of Grace learn to put their treasured traditions, their personal preferences, and their rooted relationships second to Jesus' call to feed people in Jefferson Heights.

BJ thought about the vision that members of the pastoral search team had shared with her when they were interviewing her for the position as Grace's associate pastor. It had seemed clear to her and to the search team that Grace needed to find ways to become a welcoming place for the community. But as BJ reflected on the confusion that had become evident in the incident with Charles and Deborah, she was reminded again that the journey they'd set off on was filled with more obstacles than any of them had dreamed of. She wondered if it was time to gather the leaders of Grace Church for another vision retreat.

Maybe now would be a good time to have a conversation with Bob Withey, the person who had helped Grace with the discernment process that led them to call BJ in the first place. BJ was aware of Bob's prior investment in Grace, and she respected him as a fellow pastor who had shown a lot of wisdom as a leader. She decided to give him a call.

Bob's voicemail picked up, and BJ left a message asking him to please call her back. Just a few minutes later he returned her call.

"Bob! Hi! Thanks for returning my call."

"BJ! Good to hear from you. What's up?"

"I'd like some advice, but first I need to catch you up on what's been happening here at Grace. Do you have time to talk right now, for maybe an hour or so?"

"Your timing is good. I'm all ears."

BJ brought Bob up to date on events at Grace Church over the past few months. She told him about Charles and Deborah, about Trina, about the direction in which God had been leading her.

"Bob, I'm trying to get a handle on what steps to take next to build a bridge between members of Grace and people in the Heights. I needed to talk with another pastor about everything that's been going on. Lately I've been feeling kind of like the Lone Ranger here. I remember you saying that for a lot of pastors it's really more like the Lonely Ranger, and I can really appreciate the truth of that."

"Well, I don't have any quick answers, and I know that's not what you're looking for anyway. But I do have a thought. You said you feel like you want to bounce ideas off another pastor, and I know a way you could do that. Have you heard of the local women-pastors group that Pam Dykstra plans to lead?"

"I have, but I don't know much about it."

"Pam attended training to learn how to facilitate a pastors' revitalization network. She's planning to invite a few other female pastors in the area to meet once a month to pray together and share openly about what's going on in their lives—the good stuff and the not so good stuff.

"Their goal will be to hear God's voice and follow God's leading in their ministry. Pastors I know personally who have been involved in a network like this say it's been a great help to them in their spiritual growth and as leaders of their congregations. One guy—Pam's husband, Cal, actually—tells me that the guys in his group say they're excited about ministry again, like when they first heard God's call. Let me give you Pam's number so you can get in touch if you're interested."

"Sure, Bob, give me the number." BJ wrote down Pam's name and number. "I'll have to think and pray about it before I take on another commitment, though. Listen, Bob, I should get going. I want you to know that I really appreciate you taking time to talk with me today."

"BJ, it's always a pleasure. Let me know if I can be of help in any way."

* * * * *

BJ preached a heartfelt message again that Sunday. Without using Trina's name, she told about her experiences with her over the past weeks. BJ could see that her message was connecting with some people and making others uncomfortable.

She noticed that a few people had tears in their eyes as she shared about what it would mean for Grace Church to feed Jesus' sheep.

Just as the service was drawing to a close, BJ was surprised to see Jack and June Harrison slip out a side door. They normally left through the front doors after a little polite conversation with her.

After the service, a man BJ had never seen before that day joined the line of people who wanted to say a few words to her before they left the sanctuary. He looked like he was about thirty-five and spoke with an accent that made her think he might be from India.

"Hello, Pastor. My name is Anwar. I enjoyed your message very much. I'm sure I will think about it deeply over the coming days."

"It's a pleasure to meet you, Anwar. I'm so glad you've joined us for worship today. I'm BJ Thompson. Most people call me Pastor T. Do you live nearby?"

"Yes. Just two streets east from here."

"I hope you'll come again, and maybe stop by my office sometime during the week."

BJ realized that men didn't always understand that she was only interested in getting to know them as a person seeking God's guidance and salvation. But she wanted Anwar to feel welcome. When and if it became necessary, she would make sure he understood why she was making an effort to connect with him.

"Will you be preaching again next week?"

"Yes. I preach almost every week."

"Then I will come." Anwar nodded slightly before leaving.

After most of the congregation had left for their homes in the suburbs, BJ returned to the sanctuary to grab her sermon notes. She noticed Eleanor Daly, a longtime member of Grace, sitting in one of the front pews, eyes closed and head bowed.

BJ quietly sat down across the aisle from Eleanor and began to pray silently: *Lord, thank you for this past week and the clarity*

*you gave me for the message today. Holy Spirit, I don't know what
is on Eleanor's heart right now, but I lift her up to you and ask that
you give her the words she needs to pray. Spirit, let me know how I
can give Eleanor what she might need from me.*

Eleanor opened her eyes and met BJ's gaze. "Pastor, thank you
for sharing from your heart today. Your words stirred my heart,
and I'm not sure what it's all about."

"Thank you, Eleanor. Do you have plans right now? How about
coming over to the parsonage for lunch and conversation? I was
going to eat and then go for a walk. I would love to spend some
time with you."

Eleanor hesitated just a moment before saying, "Well, thank
you. I'd love to join you."

BJ and Eleanor shared tuna sandwiches and talked about their
past and what life was like for them now. Eleanor had been married to Burt for forty years when he had suddenly passed away
from a heart attack three years ago. He had left her financially com-
fortable, but she had built her whole life around him and their two
sons. Both sons were single, lived in Los Angeles, and had careers
in the entertainment business. BJ learned that Eleanor had been
deeply depressed for two years after Burt died, and had felt mostly
just plain lost for the past year.

"It's strange, since I've always gone to church, but for the first
time in my life I feel like God is talking to me. Your sermon really
hit home. But why would God wait until I'm sixty-four?"

BJ fought the impulse to remind Eleanor that God called people
of all ages. Look at father Abraham. Or Mary and Joseph.

"Eleanor, what do you think God might be saying to you today?"

Eleanor paused. "Well, I think he wants me to help the people
you were talking about today. To join you in feeding Jesus' sheep.
To help our neighbors. But I don't know the first thing about anything like that. I've never really been out in the neighborhood. I
just walk from the parking lot to the church and back. To be honest, I would be scared to walk even one block."

"I'm planning to go for a walk this afternoon. Would you go
with me?"

Eleanor looked like she had been asked to leap onto a wild

rollercoaster. She took a deep breath. "Yes, I would!"

BJ sprang to her feet. "I know just the place we can go, and you won't even need walking shoes."

Eleanor tried on a game expression. "Well, okay. Let's go."

She followed BJ out her front door and they turned right at the sidewalk. At the first intersection, they crossed the street and turned right onto a stretch of sidewalk that ran along Hunter Park under the shade of big maple trees. It was welcome relief from the hot sun.

A few groups of young men and women were hanging out in the park listening to music or lounging on the grass under the trees. Moms watched as their kids sat on the edge of the fountain in the middle of the park, laughing and kicking water in the air.

Eleanor was quiet and watchful. They reached the end of the park and BJ pointed to a convenience store across the street. "Our destination. And you'll be glad to learn they have air conditioning and ice cream, and tables where we can sit down to enjoy both!"

A few minutes later, BJ and Eleanor pulled chairs up to a small table to eat Rocky Road and watch customers come and go. Eleanor began to relax.

"I haven't thought about it for years, but I remember Dad taking me for ice cream on Sunday afternoon. It's a nice memory. I'm having a good time now too."

BJ smiled. "Who doesn't like ice cream?"

The sun was less direct as they walked back to the church. Eleanor walked slowly and looked more closely at the sights around her. BJ knew these were literally Eleanor's first steps toward connecting with the neighborhood, but you had to start somewhere.

After going back to BJ's for Eleanor's purse, the two women walked to her car in the church parking lot. BJ gave Eleanor a hug and opened her car door. Eleanor slipped behind the wheel and looked up at BJ.

"Thank you, Pastor T. I'm sorry if I seemed scared. It's just all new territory for me."

"Thanks for being willing, and honest," said BJ. "Call me if you'd like to talk this week. I look forward to seeing you again. Let's both keep praying about what God has in store for you."

Chapter Seven

Call Waiting

The next morning BJ read her devotional and meditated on how much God had blessed her. She felt centered and at peace. "It feels great to be in your presence, Lord." She thanked God for the awakening that was clearly happening with Eleanor.

BJ and Michael had made plans to spend the day together. After lunch at BJ's, they did a little shopping and took in a movie. It was a great way to get relief from the soaring temperatures.

It was evening before Michael and BJ returned to the parsonage. A steady breeze had started to cool things off, and BJ decided to go for a short run.

BJ circled Hunter Park, and in the home stretch toward the parsonage, she spotted Trina strolling through the park with a man and another woman. BJ turned down the walkway that ran toward the fountain and jogged up to them.

"Hey, Trina!"

"Pastor T! Weird! I was just telling Chandra and Jerome about you."

"Hi, Chandra. Hi, Jerome. Nice to meet you." BJ bent forward, hands on knees, and tried to catch her breath.

"Good to see you again, Trina. Crazy-hot weather, huh?" BJ straightened up and took a long swallow from her water bottle.

Trina fanned her face with her hand. "I can barely stand my apartment. I thought I'd melt! Just the idea of cooking supper in this heat makes me faint."

BJ said, "Why don't you all come over to the church to cool off a little? My office is air conditioned, and we could order a couple of pizzas."

Jerome hung back, but Chandra jumped right in. "That would be great!"

"Okay, I just need to stop at my house—it's right next to the church. I want to ask my friend Michael to join us. Meet me on the church steps in five minutes."

BJ trotted up her front steps and burst into the living room. Michael was lying on the floor watching TV, a fan on full force.

"Hey, hon, I have a favor to ask."

"Anything, babe."

"I met Trina and a couple of her friends from the neighborhood on my run and they're joining me in my office for pizza. Will you come too?"

Michael sat up and their eyes met. "Sure. Of course. I mean, you don't know these people, really."

"I knew you'd understand."

Michael stood and stepped into his sandals. "Let's go!"

Trina, Jerome, and Chandra were waiting at the church doors. BJ introduced Michael and the two of them led the way to her office.

"Michael, will you please order the pizzas? I'll go get soda from the kitchen."

BJ could hear Michael asking what toppings everyone liked as she flipped on lights and headed downstairs to the kitchen. There were a couple liters of soda in the fridge, left over from a reception they'd held for a missionary Grace Church supported. She grabbed the soda, paper cups and plates, napkins, and a couple packages of cookies that were lying on the counter and headed back upstairs. She'd had slight misgivings about inviting two total strangers along with Trina and was relieved to hear laughter coming from her office.

BJ set paper cups on her desk and poured soda for everyone. "Jerome, Chandra, tell me a little about yourselves. Did you grow up around here?"

Chandra, a heavy-set woman in her mid-forties, seemed open and easygoing. She said she had grown up as a military brat and moved all over the country. "I've lived in the Heights for a couple of years. Right now I'm looking for work as a 'landscape engineer,'" she said with a little laugh.

BJ thought she must mean lawn or gardening work. "So you know how to garden?"

"Sure do. I trade yard work for some of my rent. If I do say so, we have the best looking yard on our block."

A look passed from Chandra to Jerome that seemed to prompt him to join in. Stocky and a little under six feet tall, he spoke with a deep voice and appeared to be about the same age as Chandra. "Well, I don't really have much to tell. I grew up on a farm near Waylon, forty miles south of here. My parents worked for a family that grew mostly corn and some beets. They gave us a place to live all the time we worked for them."

He talked about the hard work he and his brothers and sisters had done to help out in the fields and around the house. Apparently they'd all had lots of chores. "When I turned eighteen I was ready to leave the farm. Oh man, was I ready. I moved to Jefferson to work at the car parts factory that closed down a few years ago."

He said his parents had lived with him until his dad passed away a year ago. Then his mom went to live with her sister in Alabama. It seemed to BJ that he had never married.

"What keeps you busy now, Jerome?" asked Michael.

"With the economy so bad, all I've been able to land is odd jobs. I'd like to find something with regular hours and decent pay."

Trina had hardly spoken and BJ tried to draw her out a bit. "Trina, do I remember you saying you like to cook? What's your specialty?"

"I guess I can whip up some of the best fried chicken you've ever eaten. My grandma taught me her secrets when I was just a girl, and I've had lots of practice since. It's what everyone asks me to bring to a party. Chandra's really the best cook around, though. After a slice of her peach pie, you'll think you've died and gone to heaven."

"Chandra, Trina, how about if we get together to cook a meal at my place sometime?"

Just then they heard pounding on the church door. The delivery guy stepped inside and shouted, "Pizza's here!"

"Got it," said Michael. He went to pay for their order and came back with three big boxes that he placed on a side table and flipped open. "Dig in!" he said, handing plates all around.

As they loaded their plates and pulled chairs up to BJ's desk,

Chandra said, "I want to know about you, Pastor. I don't believe I've ever met a black woman who's a pastor before. How did you get to be one?"

BJ shared briefly about her upbringing and her mom and her call to Grace Church.

She tried to make it clear that while God had blessed her in many ways, she was certain it wasn't because she had specially deserved it. "One thing I do know for certain though," she added, "God has called me to serve people, all people. He put that desire in my heart, and when I'm doing that, that's when I feel like I'm doing what I was born to do."

The five of them managed to down all three pizzas. No one had room for cookies. The conversation gradually wound down and at ten-thirty BJ announced that they needed to call it a night. "It's going to be an early morning for me. But let's think about planning dinner together again. I had a great time."

"I love that idea you had earlier, getting together to make dinner," Trina said.

"That'd be great," added Jerome.

Chandra gave Jerome a good-natured poke in the ribs. "No kidding, Jerome! I know you'd really be a great help—with the eating part!"

They all got up to leave. Michael followed behind the others and switched out the lights. He was last out the door, and BJ locked up. They all walked down the steps and BJ turned to the others.

"Well, how about if we gather at my house for dinner this Saturday? Trina and I can get the groceries and start dinner. Chandra, you could come over around five-thirty to help us finish cooking and get stuff on the table. Jerome and Michael can come at six for taste testing."

They all agreed it was a date, and BJ asked Trina for her phone number. "I'll call you Saturday morning," said BJ, "and we'll go shopping."

As Trina, Chandra, and Jerome walked away from the church, it was all BJ could do to keep from jumping for joy.

She turned to Michael. "Thanks for being there this evening. It means a lot to me. I've been waiting for a time like this. It's why God called me to Grace Church—to share God's love and blessings with people who need it more than most."

"It's good to see how happy this makes you, BJ. The challenge will be to get others from the congregation to open themselves up to the same kind of relationship-building."

"I know it will be a long road to get Grace people to experience what I'm feeling right now," said BJ. "I believe it's a journey worth taking."

"Me, too, BJ. It won't be easy. But I know you're up to it!"

* * * * *

That Wednesday morning, BJ was sitting in her office reading when she heard the front doors to the church click open and shut. At first she thought it might be Trina, but then a man's voice called out, "Pastor?"

Trina rose and stepped into the hallway. It was Anwar. Even dressed in khakis and a white polo shirt, he looked only a tad less formal than he had in his Sunday suit. It was the way he held himself—squared shoulders, straight back.

"Good morning, Anwar! I'm so glad you've stopped by."

"I'm not taking you away from something important?"

"No, not at all. Well, not that what I was doing isn't important, but I always have time to visit and get to know people. Please, come to my office."

She led Anwar through the doorway and offered him a seat facing her desk. "Can I get you something to drink? Coffee? Tea?"

"Yes. I would like tea, please."

BJ pulled a tea bag from a canister, placed it in a mug, and added hot water from a carafe. "Sugar?"

"No thank you. I'll take a little milk if you have some. Otherwise just plain is fine."

BJ opened the small refrigerator she kept in her office and brought Anwar a container of half-and-half along with the mug of tea.

"Thanks so much. That's the way we drink tea in Pakistan— with milk. A habit we inherited from the British I think." Anwar smiled as he added a stream of milk to his tea.

"I was going to ask where you had grown up. How long have you been in the U.S.?"

"Not long. Just three years. I have relatives here, and a job, and I thank God I was able to get a green card. In Pakistan I worked as an engineer. But here I cannot get that kind of work, so I help my sister and brother-in-law run their restaurant. They are both educated here in the U.S. and they also are permanent residents."

"Is there anything I can do for you today, Anwar? Any questions about Grace Church that I can answer for you?"

"Well, you may be surprised to hear that my family and I are Christians. Most people when they hear we are Pakistani think we must be Muslims. They are surprised to learn that there are nearly three million Christians in our country."

"Is most of your family in Pakistan?"

"Oh, yes. My mother and father, two more sisters, one brother. My brother, Maahir, is in charge of a Christian retreat center in Punjab Province. He is the one who suggested I come to Grace Church."

"That's incredible! How could he know about this little church in Jefferson Heights?"

"Well, perhaps I should explain more carefully. You see, Maahir didn't know about this particular church, but he is familiar with your denomination. In the nineteenth century, a missionary taught many people in Pakistan about Jesus. The church my family attends today traces its roots to that missionary's time. Maahir discovered your church online. He was searching for a congregation for me that would have similar theology and teachings, and he found that yours was such a place."

"What a marvelous story! I'm so glad you've come to Grace Church."

"I am glad as well. I appreciate what you are doing to open the doors of this church to people in the community. I came here today to tell you that I will help in any way I can. If there are ways I can help, please do not hesitate to let me know."

"Thank you so much, Anwar. I'm sure I will be able to find ways for you to help. Just let me give it some thought and prayer."

"Yes, thank you, pastor. And now I must go. I have to help with lunch at the restaurant. I hope you'll stop by sometime, and I'll make you a special meal. You may find you like Pakistani food. The restaurant is Kebab Cuisine. It is just a couple of streets from here, on College Avenue. Here, I'll leave a business card and a take-out menu with you. Thank you for tea and for taking time to visit. I'll see you on Sunday, Pastor."

BJ rose along with Anwar and walked him to the door. "I'm so glad God has brought you to be part of our community. God bless you, Anwar!"

Chapter Eight

Food from the Heart

On Saturday morning, BJ went for a long run and then called Trina and invited her to go shopping to buy food for the dinner that evening.

"I'll be right over," Trina told her. True to her word, she banged on BJ's front screen door about ten minutes later.

They hopped in BJ's car and made small talk on the drive to the neighborhood grocery. It was only a couple of blocks. Normally BJ would walk to the store, pulling a handy wheeled cart that held a few bags' worth of goods. But it was just too hot today.

"What should we have to eat tonight, Trina?" BJ asked as they pulled into the store parking lot.

"I've been thinking about that. My gran taught me how to put a proper scald on chicken. Does that sound good?"

"Oh, my! Yes, it does! I forgot you told me that was your specialty. I haven't had home cooked fried chicken in months. My mouth is watering just thinking about it."

They had the shopping done and drove back to BJ's in no time. Back at the parsonage they unpacked chicken and all the fixings for a feast: collard greens, potato salad, fresh squeezed lemonade, and a pumpkin pie for dessert.

BJ made them both sandwiches for lunch and snapped open two cans of soda. Trina talked about all her good memories of her gran as they ate, and she had a lot of questions for BJ about her life, her faith, and her mom.

They talked for a couple of hours, and BJ felt like she needed a short rest before jumping into preparations for the evening. "Trina, I'm going to go upstairs and lie down for about a half hour. The heat is getting to me just a little, and I have the air on up there. Do you want to just hang out while I rest?"

"Sure. I don't mind. And I can get started with dinner if that's okay with you."

"That would be great. Here, let's move these floor fans from the living room into the kitchen to give you some relief."

After moving the fans and telling Trina where to find what she needed in the kitchen, BJ climbed the stairs to her bedroom. She knew she might be taking a chance leaving Trina downstairs alone. She still didn't know the young woman very well. But she also believed that most people rise to the level of expectation that is put on them. She also figured this was the way she would want to be treated if the situation were reversed.

The hum of the air conditioner lulled her to sleep in no time. As was her habit, she dozed for a half-hour or so and woke up refreshed. BJ had been taking reenergizing cat naps for years.

The tantalizing smell of chicken frying welcomed BJ back to the kitchen. Trina stood at the stove, turning the flour-and-spice-coated pieces in the fry pan. She turned and smiled. "This is a nice kitchen to cook in."

"I'm glad you're finding what you need. The chicken smells great! How about if I start the potato salad?"

"Sure! I've already microwaved the potatoes. They're in the fridge along with all the other fixings."

BJ and Trina made small talk as they finished preparing dinner. Out of the blue, Trina asked, "Pastor T, why are you so nice to me?"

BJ stopped stirring the pitcher of lemonade she was making and looked over at Trina. "Two reasons: one, because I know that God wants me to love everyone, just as God loves me. I know that in God's eyes you are his beloved child just the same as I am. And two, as I'm getting to know you, I just plain like you."

Trina looked away, and BJ thought she might be ashamed that she had teared up. "Pastor T, you don't know me."

"Trina, you are my sister. Maybe you've done some things you aren't proud of, but you and I are pretty much the same...daughters of the same God. I believe you deserve to be loved by your sister. It's that simple."

A tear spilled down Trina's cheek. BJ walked over and hugged her. Trina started to pull away, but then she relaxed and a flood of tears broke loose. BJ gave Trina a tighter hug and then stepped back and held Trina's hand for a moment before walking over to the kitchen counter to grab a fistful of tissues for her. "Besides, if that aroma is anything to go by, you make the most heavenly fried chicken in the Heights!"

Trina's smile was back. "Thanks, Pastor T."

She took the tissues BJ offered, wiped her eyes, and took a deep breath. "Well, everyone will be here in just a few minutes, won't they?"

BJ looked at the clock above the sink. "Wow. Where did the time go? Let's see. I'll set the table. Here's a bowl for the potato salad. We're almost ready for them."

"Ready or not, here I come," Chandra called out as she came through the back door into the kitchen. "I brought a couple bottles of soda. Hope it's what you like."

"Thanks, Chandra. Perfect!" said BJ. "It's the one thing I forgot to pick up." She put the soda in the fridge and then she and Chandra and Trina hustled to get everything ready before Jerome and Michael got there.

Michael and Jerome arrived at the same time, and BJ teased them for showing up just in time to eat.

"Please, everyone, have a seat," said BJ. She started to pray. "Loving, gracious God, thank you for the many blessings we experience by being together and by sharing this food that you have provided. In Jesus' holy name we pray. Amen!"

During the meal and afterward, BJ kept the conversation flowing, asking Trina, Chandra, and Jerome what gave them joy in life, what they were like as kids, what movies made them laugh, and what was going on in the neighborhood. She could tell that Chandra and Jerome cared deeply about their friends and neighbors in the Heights and did what they could to help them over rough patches in their lives.

As the evening wrapped up BJ asked them if they could think of ways that Grace Church could be present with people in the community. Chandra looked thoughtful. "I'm not sure what a church like Grace could do. I don't mean to offend, but I don't think many people here feel like Grace is really part of the Heights scene, if you know what I mean."

"That's right," said Jerome. "If it's just a bunch of the rich folks trying to make themselves feel better by helping some of the poor folks, well, that's not going to fly."

"I totally agree," said BJ. "I apologize if I didn't express myself clearly. I'd like to find ways for Grace people and neighborhood people to actually get to know each other and help each other. I'm confident that God has given every person gifts and abilities. If there is to be a bridge between Grace and the people of the Heights, it has to be a two-way bridge that's built by all of the people. Otherwise it won't be of any real use at all."

Jerome and Chandra seemed to accept BJ's insights. They said they would think about the bridge-building possibilities.

BJ divided the leftovers to send home with her guests. Chandra and Jerome left around eight and Michael just a little later, but Trina stayed and talked with BJ for another two hours.

During their conversation, Trina revealed that her boyfriend was really more like her pimp, just as BJ had feared.

"I know you're afraid. Would you go with me to check out the women's shelter? They could help you find a different way to live, Trina. You are so gifted. You have so much to offer. Would you at least think about it?"

Trina said she would. Before Trina left, BJ asked to pray with her. "God, bless Trina. Show her your plan for her life."

BJ spoke directly to Trina. "You've told me how your grandma brought you to church when you were little, and how you remember giving your life to Jesus all those years ago. Trina, Jesus has never left you, and he's with you now. Do you believe that?"

"Yes, I do."

"Then, Trina, just talk to him like you did when you were little. God will guide you and show you what to do next."

BJ prayed again. "Lord, help my sister hear your voice and give her strength to follow you and to love you as she did when she was just a child. Thank you for this evening, Lord. Please be with each of us over the coming days, and work in our hearts to bring us closer to you. I praise your holy name. Amen."

Trina said, "Amen."

BJ saw tears in Trina's eyes again. The two women hugged. "Go with God, Trina."

"I will. Thank you for everything, Pastor T. Good night!" Trina hugged BJ again before walking out the door. She turned and gave BJ a wave and a smile before crossing the street. BJ watched until she reached the intersection, turned left, and disappeared around the corner.

BJ hummed praise songs as she cleaned up the kitchen. She watched the late news, and did a quick review of her sermon for the next morning. She got ready for bed, crawled in, prayed with thanks for all that had happened that evening, and fell into a deep sleep.

* * * * *

That Sunday, BJ took Mark 8:34-35 (NIV) as her text:

> Then [Jesus] called the crowd to him along with his disci-
> ples and said: "Whoever wants to be my disciple must
> deny themselves and take up their cross and follow
> me. For whoever wants to save their life will lose it, but
> whoever loses their life for me and for the gospel will save
> it.

She talked about Jesus' radical message of dying to self—about giving away your life that you may gain life—all in the context of the members of Grace Church becoming a welcoming community for their neighbors.

"I acknowledge that some people will not want to go on this journey of giving their life over to God. Some people will fight this, and maybe not in very Christian ways. We must be prepared to face these challenges. I certainly intend to face them as long as the core body of Grace is on board."

Afterward several key people took time to let her know they were indeed "on board." Their support helped her feel ready to face the challenges that were bound to keep popping up. She invited each person who had encouraged her to join her as a leader on the journey...not just a follower.

Chapter Nine

Crossing Jordan

On Monday BJ woke with the sunrise and got an early start on the day. She pulled on a tank top, shorts, and running shoes, grabbed a water bottle, and left the house to get in a long run while it was still relatively cool.

Traffic filled the streets, but the park and sidewalks were fairly empty and she made good time. As BJ turned a corner to head toward home she heard an emergency vehicle siren wail in the distance. The sound grew louder for several minutes and then shut down. BJ jogged several more blocks and noticed that traffic wasn't moving through the intersection ahead.

As she usually did, BJ started praying for the people the EMTs were there to help. At the cross street she slowed to a walk and looked to the right, where the ambulance had pulled over in front of a three-story apartment building. The sound of another siren drew closer. A police cruiser turned the corner and parked across the street from the apartment building. Two officers sprinted into the building, holsters open, hands on their gun grips.

BJ walked slowly toward the group of neighbors who were gathering in front of the building that the EMTs and two officers had run into. As she grew close BJ heard a woman sobbing. "I just had dinner with her last night!" It was Chandra.

Oh, no. Trina.

BJ would remember the next few hours as a series of images caught in bright late-morning light.

The medical examiner walking up the steps and into the building.

A body bag being carried out with Trina's small body inside.

Chandra and another woman hugging and crying.

Officers tying off the area with yellow tape.

A detective took down BJ's name, address, and phone number and asked if she knew Trina and if she knew of anyone who might want to harm her. BJ told the officer about the bruises and that Trina wouldn't tell who had hurt her. The detective asked whether BJ would be home later in the day, and if she could stop by to ask a few more questions.

BJ said that would be fine. She walked over to Chandra. "Chandra, I'm so, so sorry." Chandra nodded and they hugged. "Please, please, let me know if there is any way I can be of help. I would be willing to preach at her service, if that's what her family needs. I'll be home all day. Walk over anytime if you want to talk, okay?" Chandra nodded again.

BJ's legs felt like lead as she walked home. She asked God to comfort Trina's friends and to bring something good out of this awful event.

As she walked BJ began to ask herself questions: *Did I do something that may have brought this on? Because of my encouragement, did Trina try to go to a shelter and get caught by her pimp? Is there something I could have done that I didn't do?*

Lord, help me to turn this over to you. And help me to know what you would have me do at this tragic time.

BJ phoned Michael and her mom to tell them the sad news and to talk over her doubts about her own role in the tragedy. Both offered to come over right away. BJ appreciated their offers, but told them she had more calls to make. And besides, she didn't want too many people around that afternoon. It might intimidate Chandra if she decided to drop by.

The detective stopped by briefly, but BJ didn't have anything to add to her earlier statement. She had her suspicions about Trina's "boyfriend" but nothing concrete to back them up.

Mid-afternoon BJ made calls to Eleanor and Charles and Deborah. She told them what had happened and asked if they would be willing to help if Chandra or others from the community asked her to perform Trina's funeral service. They all said yes without hesitation. They would support BJ in any way they could.

BJ remembered Anwar's offer to help open Grace Church up to the community. She dug through her briefcase for the business

card he had given her for the restaurant where he worked for his
sister and brother-in-law. The woman who answered her call put
Anwar on the line. He readily agreed to help as well, and he
thought his sister and her husband might be willing to send food,
too. He would find out and get back to her.

After making the calls, BJ dropped into one of her living room
armchairs. Tears welled up from deep inside. She reached for a
Bible that lay on the table beside her and turned to 1 Corinthians
15:55-57: "Where, O death, is your victory? Where, O death, is
your sting? The sting of death is sin, and the power of sin is the
law. But thanks be to God! He gives us the victory through our
Lord Jesus Christ."

BJ heard a soft knock at the front door and rose to answer it.
Chandra stood just beyond the screen door with Jerome a few steps
behind her on the walkway.

"Chandra, Jerome. Please, come in." They stepped into BJ's living room. Chandra's eyes were puffy from crying. Jerome looked
angry.

"Please, sit down. Can I get you something to drink?" BJ thought
of the lemonade left over from the dinner they'd all shared with
Trina just hours ago. She wouldn't be able to serve that. Just thinking about it filled her eyes with tears.

"No thanks, Pastor T," said Jerome. "I saw the police stop by
here earlier. Were they asking about Trina?"

"Yes. A detective wanted to know if I had any idea who would
want to hurt Trina. Of course I'd noticed all the bruises on her, and
I told the officer about that. But Trina never told me straight out
who was hurting her, so I really didn't have much to offer."

Jerome stood up again. "It had to be that no good son of a
bitch...that so-called boyfriend of hers. I warned Trina about mess-
ing with that piece of shit." He paused and then added, "I'm sorry,
Preacher, I can't remember when I've been this mad. He just better
pray we don't meet up. I swear I'll..." Suddenly the steam just
went out of Jerome. He collapsed back in his chair and just stared
at the floor.

"Trina seemed like a daughter to me since her mom died,"
Chandra said softly. "I love that girl so much!" She began sobbing

and BJ rose to hand her a box of tissues. BJ went over and kneeled in front of Chandra and covered Chandra's hands with her own. "Trina meant a lot to me, too, even in the short time we knew each other."

"Thank you, Pastor." Chandra sighed and looked up at BJ. "Did you mean what you said about helping with the funeral? That would be so nice. I know Trina thought a lot of you too, even if you just met. She said it seemed like you knew each other a lot longer than just a few weeks. I think you helped her remember who she really was, what she really wanted out of life. Trina was such a bright flower before life brought her low. She talked about starting over, a new beginning, but now she'll never get the chance." Chandra's last few words came out in a whisper as she broke down again.

"I believe God brought us together for a reason," BJ said softly. Inwardly she thought that although this time of darkness seemed like the end, God was mightier than that. God could take even something as tragic as this and bring good out of it. BJ rose from the floor and went back to her seat across from Chandra. "I would be honored to preach at Trina's funeral, and I've already called a few people from the church. They want to help all they can, too."

Chandra took a few tissues and wiped her eyes and blew her nose. "That would be a help. I know lots of people who will want to pay their respects. Trina has…Trina had…lots of friends. Jerome's brother and sister sing and play music at their church. I'm sure they'll want to help too."

"That's right," Jerome said as though the thought had just occurred to him. "I'll talk to them right away." He stood and walked out the front door and began making calls.

"Now tell me about Trina," said BJ to Chandra. "I want to know all about her before I preach."

Chandra told BJ everything she could think of. Trina had been one of those people who could tell stories and make everyone laugh, and just remembering those times made Chandra smile.

"Chandra, could you tell a few of those stories about Trina at the service? You seem to know her better than anyone. It would be a way to honor her."

"Yes, I want to do that. I will miss Trina every day," she said as her tears flowed again.

Jerome walked in. "It's all set. Delia and Davis will sing and play at the service. Pastor T, here are their phone numbers so you can work out the times and everything."

"Thanks, Jerome. I'll preach, Chandra will tell about Trina's life, your brother and sister will provide music, and folks from Grace Church have offered to serve food and help any way they can."

"Preacher, we'll leave you to get started on your message," Jerome said. Chandra followed him to the door and turned to BJ. "We're going to see if we can raise money in the neighborhood for the burial. Thanks for all you're doing to help."

BJ asked how many people from the neighborhood might come to the service. Chandra said she thought maybe seventy-five to a hundred.

After they'd left, BJ sat down on the couch. She felt bone tired, but there was a lot to do. She leaned on the armrest, closed her eyes, and prayed for direction and the energy to keep moving.

BJ called Deborah and asked her to coordinate ordering, cooking, and serving food for about a hundred guests. Then Anwar called to say he would bring enough chicken and rice to feed about fifty people and that he would also be happy to help serve. BJ put him in touch with Deborah.

BJ made one more call, this time to Ally's Place. Ally answered the phone and the sadness in her voice told BJ that she knew all about Trina. Before BJ asked for her support, Ally said, "Trina, bless her soul, she came in here a lot. Do you know if there's anything her family needs?"

BJ filled Ally in on the funeral plans. "It would be great if you could help Anwar and the others after the service."

"I sure will. I'll be happy to bring more food too. How about if you give me Anwar's number and we can work out what I need to bring."

"Thanks so much, Ally. I really appreciate that. I'm so tired I can't think straight."

BJ had just gotten off the phone with Ally when Michael called to say he would be bringing dinner over to her place in about an hour, "I won't stay long. I know you need time to work on the service."

"Thanks, Michael. Thanks for your support and understanding. I don't know how much I'll feel like eating, but your thoughtfulness means a lot to me."

Chapter Ten

Soon and Very Soon

Tuesday morning BJ walked over to her office to continue working on her message for Trina's funeral. She also needed to know which day to hold the memorial. She called the police, who put her in touch with the medical examiner's office. BJ learned that an autopsy was being performed, since the death was suspicious. Trina's body would be released to a local mortuary the next day.

BJ called Chandra and learned that she and Jerome had raised five hundred dollars to put toward the cost of a casket. The funeral home would allow them a couple of months to come up with another one thousand dollars to pay the rest of the expenses. Chandra would arrange for Trina's body to be brought to the church Thursday morning.

* * * * *

As BJ looked out over the crowd of people filling the pews for Trina's funeral, she was amazed at how many people from the neighborhood had turned out. The church's roadside sign had announced the funeral service for the past day and a half. In spite of her deep sadness, BJ was blessed to see that in response to a message that went out on Grace Church's prayer tree, quite a few people from Grace had come too. Some were sitting in the pews, and she knew that others were downstairs helping Deborah, Anwar, and Ally with the food for afterward. Half a dozen Grace folks had sent flowers, and combined with those from neighborhood people, they filled the steps to the pulpit, framing Trina's casket.

"Welcome," BJ began. "All of us are gathered here today to honor Trina Johnson—a young woman with a huge heart and a huge family here in the Heights. It says a lot about Trina that so many people are here today. Those who knew her best know that in the past few weeks, Trina made some important decisions. She was changing the direction of her life. She had reconnected with God's love for her and the plan God had for her life. She had a renewed vision for what her life could be.

"Trina and I met less than a month ago. But we saw each other often and had long talks about life, about dreams, about hope. You might be thinking that now it seems like, what was the point? She's gone. She won't have a chance to live that new life.

"Friends, if I thought that was true, I'd feel nothing but sadness. All hope would die. But I don't believe all is lost. In fact, I am sure that Trina's story and legacy are just beginning."

BJ shared briefly about Trina's recommitment to faith. "I have every confidence that our sister Trina is in the arms of her loving God in heaven. And that she will live forever."

Chandra somehow held it together as she talked about Trina. BJ thought Chandra got it just right, balancing stories of the happy and sad times in Trina's life, the humor and the dark side, the tears and the triumph. Trina's friends responded with a mix of tears and laughter.

Jerome's brother Davis accompanied their sister Delia for a spirited rendition of "Soon and Very Soon," by Andrae Crouch and the Disciples. Everyone joined in for "Go Tell It on the Mountain." Even if it was usually sung at Christmas, it was a song almost everyone was familiar with, and it seemed right.

Many people came up to BJ after the service to tell her that they were moved by her message. Nearly everyone stayed for food and conversation in the church basement afterward. As BJ watched people eat and talk together, she felt more than ever that she would do whatever it took to break down the walls between Grace and the Heights. She felt certain that the key would be for people in the congregation to understand that they had to form meaningful relationships with neighborhood folks. They needed to become aware of how they came across to those people and be willing not just to serve them, but to be served by them.

BJ ended the day fully aware of God's love, God's grace, and God's salvation and also fully aware of a new hole in her heart. A little piece of her had died with Trina. A line from John Donne came to mind: "Send not to know for whom the bell tolls, it tolls for thee."

She went off to bed feeling tired, sad, and yet richly blessed.

Chapter Eleven
The Jesus Way

That Sunday, BJ preached on John chapter 4, the story of the Samaritan woman at the well.

"At the well in Samaria," she began, "Jesus met a woman who had had five husbands and was currently living with a man who wasn't her husband. In that day and age her behavior made her a social reject, a complete outsider. She visited the community well to get water at the hottest part of the day because that was the only time when other women would not be there. The other women in her community would have scorned and ridiculed her, picked on her, made fun of her. She went alone to the well, and there was Jesus. And this is interesting: he served her by asking her to serve him.

"Jesus was completely aware of the impact that his words and actions would have on this woman. He's a Jewish male, and Jewish men had nothing to do with Samaritan women. He's a rabbi, a Jewish religious teacher, and a rabbi would not have had anything to do with women who had had multiple husbands. Jesus knew that if he just started talking to her, she'd be so shocked she would just run away. She would hear nothing of the freedom Jesus wanted to offer her. So Jesus simply sits down and says, 'Can you get me some water?'

"People who live on the edges of society, who know what it feels like to be overlooked and mistreated and misunderstood, will be attracted to our faith community only if we follow Jesus' example. He annihilated the barriers between Jew and Samaritan with a simple request. He treated this woman who was an outcast with the same dignity and respect he would have exhibited toward any of the women of his own community.

"Friends, when we reach out to others, it's really important to

be aware of how we come across to them. If we want to truly love
our neighbors and if we want them to be open to receiving the
good news of Jesus Christ, then we need be open to ways that we
can receive from those people as well.

"We need to affirm their dignity and worth in the eyes of our
loving God. And by the way, most of them have many things to
teach us about justice, love, community, and so much more. We
need to understand what matters to them and what's going on in
their lives. Jesus knew everything going on in the Samaritan
woman's life because he is God. We must learn these things by developing relationships, which sometimes become friendships. We
must invite people into our homes and our lives and our hearts."

* * * * *

After the service, Eleanor remained in her pew praying. When
most of the others had left, BJ walked over to Eleanor and sat down
just a few feet away. Eleanor opened her eyes. "I get it," she said. "I
understand what you're telling us, even if I haven't fully experienced it yet."

BJ reached out and took Eleanor's hand. "I know you get it."

"I suspect you know what's going on inside of me," Eleanor
said.

"I think I have an idea," BJ said, "but talk with me about what
you're thinking and feeling right now."

Eleanor said, "I don't know what exactly is going to happen, but
I know for certain that I'm ready to follow you into this neighborhood, Pastor Barbara. It still seems risky, but I know I'm supposed
to do it, so I'm not afraid. What can I do to help change this congregation so that we show God's love to our neighbors?"

"What is God telling you to do, Eleanor?"

"I think it starts with just meeting some of the neighbors. I want
to learn who they are. I want to find out how I might bless them.
And I like what you said about Jesus and the woman at the well. I
want to follow his example, and be open to the people from the
neighborhood serving me too."

"Praise God, Eleanor! Can I pray with you a moment?"

"Sure." They held hands and bowed their heads.

"Loving and gracious God, thank you that you choose sinners

like us to spread your love and good news. Thank you that you
have led me here to Grace Church. Thank you that you have led
my sister Eleanor to realize your love. Let her be your instrument
in sharing it with our neighbors. Lord, it's obvious that you are at
work here and we long to join you. Give us ears to hear, eyes to
see, and hearts to feel what you are telling us. Lord, I lift up
Eleanor and ask that you bless her in ways so rich she won't be
able to explain them with words, just like you have done with me.
Thank you for your love, your grace, your mercy, and your Holy
Spirit. Jesus, it's in your precious name we pray. Amen."

Eleanor gave BJ a quick hug. "Thank you."

"Eleanor, did you happen to meet Chandra and Jerome at Trina's
memorial service?"

"I did. They both came downstairs to thank all of us who were
serving food that day."

"I'm planning to meet soon with both of them to talk about starting a weekly community meeting that would include a time for
prayer and maybe a short devotion. If they agree, would you come
too?

"I would love to!"

"Great! I'll get back to you to let you know when and where we
plan to meet."

"That would be lovely. I'm available to come just about any day
and any time. It's not like I have a lot on my schedule these days."

"And there's one more thing I've been meaning to talk about
with you, Eleanor. Grace needs another person on the leadership
council. I'd really like it to be a woman. Would you consider joining? I know God is stirring in your heart to help move Grace into
the community. The council could use some of that stirring, too."

"Oh my, I'm not sure. It sounds like a huge responsibility."

"I'm confident that you would do a great job, Eleanor. And I
would be there to support and mentor you all the way."

"I'm honored that you've asked me, and I'll certainly pray about
it."

"Thanks, Eleanor. I'll pray too. And I'll get in touch soon about
the Bible study."

Eleanor smiled as she rose to go. "I have a roast in the oven,

Pastor. I'd better get a move on before it's dry as the Sahara!"

* * * * *

The following Wednesday, BJ left the parsonage shortly after breakfast and was mentally going over her plans for the day as she walked over to the church. First on her to-do list was placing calls to Chandra and Jerome. She invited them to stop by the parsonage for lunch. She wanted to talk with them about starting a weekly community meeting focused on ways neighborhood people and Grace Church people could begin to build meaningful relationships, with an eye toward doing ministry together. She also made a few quick visits to two Grace Church members who were recovering from serious surgery.

Lunch with Jerome and Chandra went well. They talked at length about the big hole Trina's death had left in their lives. The three of them revisited how things had gone at her funeral.

BJ brought up her idea of weekly community meetings and asked Chandra if she would be willing to hold them in her home. Chandra agreed, and she and Jerome offered to invite a few neighborhood people that they thought might be interested. BJ said she would ask Anwar and Eleanor to come. Jerome and Chandra also agreed that BJ could open the meetings with a short devotional and offer to lead them all in prayer.

To BJ it seemed like real progress toward building a Grace-Heights bridge. The journey ahead was sure to be filled with bumps and potholes, but BJ sensed that at last things were inching forward.

After Chandra and Jerome left, BJ decided to go back to the church. She had to answer emails and phone calls, make more hospital visits, and work on Sunday's message. But she also was energized to start planning her devotional for the first community-church get-together, which was planned for the following Wednesday. It would have to be engaging without being preachy. She smiled at the name Jerome had said he wanted to give the meetings: "Grace in the Heights."

As BJ stepped into her office, she noticed a handwritten note on the seat of her chair. Picking it up, she saw it was signed by Jack Harrison, one of the members of the leadership council.

Pastor Barbara, I am very concerned about how things are
going around here and where you seem to be leading us. I
know that we need change, but not this change. You are
being reckless with your personal agenda to reach out to
the people you love with no regard for those we have been
called to love.

BJ paused for a quick prayer and kept reading:

Our family has decided to leave Grace and find a church
that is more relevant to how we see Christianity, a church
that is more aligned with our view of the world.

This pains us as we have been attending Grace for almost
thirty years but we can't be a part of where you are leading
this church. I thought you at least should know why we're
leaving. Please consider this note my resignation from the
executive council and our resignation from the membership of Grace. If you have a change of heart, you can contact me and talk about what needs to happen if we are to
return.

"Here we go again," BJ said aloud. But this time BJ grabbed her
planner and looked up the number Bob Withey had given her for
Pam Dykstra.

Pam's voicemail picked up the call, so BJ left a short message
asking Pam to get in touch, and adding that she wanted to learn
about the group Pam planned to lead for women pastors in the
area.

BJ walked back to the parsonage. The energy from her meeting
with Chandra and Jerome had been replaced with a feeling of im-
mense weariness. She sat on her living room couch and laid her
head on the armrest. No thoughts, no rational perspective. She was
angry, then hurt, then angry again. BJ reached for her phone and
called Johanna.

Johanna knew from BJ's flat "Hello, Mom" that something was
terribly wrong. "What happened, baby?"

BJ told Johanna about the note from Jack.

"I'm sorry to hear that you're going through that with another member of the congregation, and especially a member of the leadership council. But you seem much calmer this time."

"It's true, although I have to say it feels more like depression. But at the same time, I am encouraged to see so much progress too—with Eleanor, and with Chandra and Jerome. With the way Grace folks pulled together to support Trina's funeral. That helps a lot."

"We've always known it would be tough to bring Grace and Heights people together. But it's often tough to do the right thing, to follow God's leading, isn't it?"

The two of them talked for half an hour, and when her conversation with Johanna ended BJ decided she needed to focus on things that would cheer her up. She would deal with Jack later. She called and invited Michael over for dinner. They spent the rest of the afternoon and evening together, cooking, eating, watching a movie—just enjoying each other's company.

Around seven that evening, Pam Dykstra returned BJ's call. BJ and Pam had met at a few church gatherings over the years, but never one-on-one. They agreed it was high time, and made plans to meet for lunch at Ally's on Friday.

Chapter Twelve

Partners in Ministry

On Thursday, BJ got up at five o'clock to have time for a long run. Traffic was just beginning to pick up. As BJ jogged through the park, she thought about Trina and felt sad that their budding friendship had not had a chance to grow. She also thought about the previous day—the meeting with Chandra and Jerome, the message from Jack, her time with Michael, her conversation with Pam. What a day!

When BJ got back to the parsonage it was after seven. She did a few stretches, sipped juice and nibbled toast while scanning the paper, and took a quick shower.

Her first order of business was to contact Jack Harrison to have another "healthy conflict" conversation. She had come to believe what author Susan Scott wrote in her book *Fierce Conversations*— you need to tackle your toughest problems first.

As she did before her talk with Charles, she reviewed the "Leaning into Healthy Conflict" model. She recalled a saying her mother often repeated: "Truth without love is mean, and love without truth is a lie." She wanted above all to speak the truth in love, and in her conversation with Jack she knew she would need to hold on to that desire with all her heart.

She said a prayer and called Jack's number. He picked up.

"Hello, Jack, this is Pastor Barbara."

"Hi, Pastor."

"I received the note you left on my desk, and I need to talk with you about it."

"So are you rethinking what you've been doing?"

"No, not exactly. But I think we should get together face to face so I can better understand where you're coming from and share with you where I'm coming from."

"No, I don't think we'll be getting together. We can talk on the phone if you feel the need to talk."

"Okay. Then please tell me more about why you wrote the note and why you are suggesting you will leave Grace."

"I wrote because I believe you deserve to know we are leaving, so you don't wonder why we're suddenly gone. And we're leaving for the reasons I mentioned in the note."

BJ kept her cool. "Please tell me more about what you meant when you wrote about wanting to find a more relevant church."

"You know what I mean."

"No, I honestly don't. Please explain."

Jack seemed taken aback for a moment. "I mean a church that reaches out to people in other neighborhoods, like where *we* live."

"Do you believe I'm asking you to not reach out to people in your own neighborhood?"

"Well, no, but you never mention that as a possibility. All you talk about is your people in Jefferson Heights."

"Jack, what do you mean by 'your people'"?

Jack's voice rose. "Pastor, you know exactly what I mean. I mean your 'people of color' as you like to be called these days."

Wow! Face to face with racism. Or at least ear to ear. BJ knew she had the right to blast him, to remind him in no uncertain terms that the Bible clearly says we are all brothers and sisters. That it is clearly a sin to look down on any neighbor because of the color of that person's skin. And a substantial part of her really *wanted* to blast him. But her mother's words echoed in her heart: "Truth without love is mean."

"Jack, now I understand perfectly. I consider your comments to be racist, and frankly I expected better of you. So I was confused by your note, but now it is clear. We will miss you, Jack. I pray that God opens your..."

Jack hung up before she could say "heart."

She took a deep breath. She was angry, surprised, hurt, and also proud that she had held it together. She decided she needed to share this with the leadership team, but she wasn't sure how.

The more she thought about the note and conversation with Jack Harrison, the more BJ was beginning to believe it was an indication that the necessary changes at Grace Church were on track. She knew from her leadership training and experiences that when you drive substantive changes you will most likely lose people along the way.

She also knew that it's a blessing to lose the "right people" along the way. She was sad about losing some members of the Harrison family, but not Jack. Racism is poison in any congregation. If Jack couldn't see his attitude was racist and repent of that hideous sin, he was no longer welcome at Grace Church.

BJ realized that Jack actually had saved her from having to take disciplinary action down the road. God's hand was in this. It was on her, on Grace Church, and on this neighborhood in the Heights.

"God, thank you for your leadership, for your wisdom, for your love and mercy," she prayed. "I will trust you from here on out—again—and I know you will give me and all of us everything we need to love our neighbors as we love you. Thank you, Jesus. It's in your name I pray. Amen."

* * * * *

That afternoon, Eleanor stopped by BJ's office to tell her that although she still didn't feel like she was qualified, she was willing to become a member of the leadership council. BJ hugged her and then told her about Jack's note and his plans to leave the council and Grace Church.

BJ said if Jack followed through, she would like to move immediately to bring Eleanor onto the team. Eleanor was surprised things were moving so quickly, but BJ was grateful that Eleanor also said she could sense God's hand in all that had happened and was still willing to serve.

Chapter Thirteen

My Cup Runneth Over

Friday, just before noon, BJ walked into Ally's Place for lunch with Pam.

"Hi, Ally. How are you today?" BJ said with a big smile.

"If I was any better I think I'd burst! How about you, Pastor T?"

"Well, I have to say I've had some ups and some downs. Still, I can hardly wait for God to write the next chapter."

"Well that's finer than the tiny diamond on my first engagement ring."

"How many of those rings have you had, Ally?"

"Too many to mention," she said with a wry grin. Just then Pam walked in. She held out her hand. "Hello, Barbara. I'm so glad we're finally going to get to know each other."

"Hello, Pam. I've looked forward to this too." BJ introduced Pam and Ally. "Ally, Pam and her husband are pastors at First Church, just a few miles from here."

"It's good to meet another lady pastor, Pastor Pam. I know Pastor T is doing a lot of good for people here in the Heights. You come on back to the booth here in the corner. It's nice and private—a good place to talk."

Ally handed BJ and Pam menus and left them to decide what to order.

Pam leaned across the Formica-topped table. "Barbara, I sense God has brought us together. It's very exciting!"

"I feel it too!" said BJ. "And please, call me BJ. That's what all my friends call me."

"BJ, I'm just starting to build a network of female pastors in Jefferson Heights. Half a dozen of us share a common interest in urban ministry, which you know better than most can be a huge challenge. I want us to meet about once a month to pray together, share our experiences, and just plain encourage each other. I would so love it if you'd consider becoming a charter member of the network."

BJ and Pam spent the next two hours talking about their past, their families, their congregations, and what a pastors network might be like for the six women pastors in the Jefferson Heights area.

Pam shared how she would set up the network. She told BJ the focus would be on supporting each other. The women would also challenge each other to grow as pastors and in every area of their lives. They would help each other grow more quickly into the people God had created them to be.

Pam also shared how each woman would be coached one-on-one by someone who had been trained to help her think through ideas and roadblocks that might get in the way of this growth.

She added that besides Pam and BJ, four other urban pastors would probably be joining the network: Maria Garcia of Iglesia Comunidad, Jennifer Poll of City Church, Inez Little Bear, the chaplain at the local homeless shelter, and Lynda Feldt, a chaplain at Jefferson City Hospital.

BJ had met Maria a few times, and she knew Jennifer and Inez by reputation. The more BJ learned about the network the more excited she became. Finally she asked, "When can we start?"

"Well, if you're willing to have me be your coach, we could start as soon as you like.

BJ said, "That sounds great. What would you like me to do next?"

Pam said, "I've placed calls to Inez, Maria, and Jennifer. And I've already connected with Lynda, who is also trained as a coach. Lynda will help me with the leadership and coaching. She and I plan to meet with Jennifer, Maria, and Inez. Would you be willing to talk with them too, so all of us can get a better sense of who the others are?"

BJ said, "Sure, I would happy to. Give them my contact information and ask them to call me or stop by my office."

"Great!" said Pam. "Lynda and I will let you know what to

expect next right after we meet with the other women. In the meantime, you and I can schedule our first coaching session and get started with that."

BJ and Pam got out their calendars and set their first coaching session for the following Wednesday at ten in the morning.

"BJ, I'm thrilled that this network seems like it's actually going to come together. I really feel that the Holy Spirit is directing all of this."

BJ said, "It sounds like a great way for all of us to learn from each other and support each other. Thanks so much for taking the lead in this."

They ended with a brief prayer of thanksgiving, paid for their food, and stood to leave. They gave each other a quick hug, and Pam headed out the door, waving good-bye to Ally.

Ally winked at BJ. "What have you two got planned? Your voices were all twittery. I thought maybe you were talking about a hot new boyfriend. But we both know men don't come any better than your Michael!"

"Ally, Michael's shrimp gumbo is almost as good as yours. I would be crazy to mess things up with a man like that!"

"Well, I've leave the deep discussions about God to you and your pastor friend. But you know, good things happen when you lunch at Ally's."

"You've got that right, Ally. You've got that right for sure. Sort of like what happens when people visit my place. Everyone sure appreciated all your help with the food at Trina's funeral. I hope you stop by again real soon. There's a community group that will start meeting at Chandra's soon. You might want to check that out."

Ally said she'd talk with Chandra about coming to the meetings. After goodbyes, BJ walked back to the church with the pop song "Walking in Memphis" running through her head. The lyrics were about feeling like you were walking with your feet ten feet off the ground. She starting humming the tune, and a line from the song stuck in her mind: "But do I really feel the way I feel?" She felt so encouraged after her meeting with Pam, but would the promise that seemed to be offered by the network turn out to be real?

She continued humming as she walked. "Walking in Memphis"

morphed into an old-time hymn, and then BJ began singing out
loud: "Praise God from whom all blessings flow..."

The glow from her meeting with Pam stayed with BJ throughout
the afternoon. In the background though was the nagging thought
that next Tuesday evening she would have to tell the leadership
council about Jack Harrison's note, their conversation, and his de-
parture.

* * * * *

Tuesday evening rolled around in no time. Most of the members
of the leadership council heartily affirmed her handling of the situation with Jack, even though it was hard to lose a member of their
team this way. BJ noted that Bill Harder, the council vice president, was quiet and distant.

Over the next three weeks two more families left the church,
echoing the Harrisons' sentiments. In both cases BJ followed up
with a phone call and both times became convinced that under-
tones of racism were at play. Even in light of that reality, their leaving had power to shock and hurt her. She kept reminding herself
that you don't always know what's really in someone's heart until
that person is challenged by a situation or a leader. In spite of
these difficult and hurtful realities she was not moved an inch
from her clear call to communicate God's direction to the remain-
ing members of Grace and the people of the Heights.

Chapter Fourteen

God's Vision for Grace Revealed

A week after their lunch at Ally's, Pam and BJ started their coaching relationship. BJ quickly came to realize that her mother had been coaching her all along by asking great questions, listening carefully, and occasionally throwing out an idea to consider.

Over the next months Pam helped BJ clarify her thinking about the need to hold another vision retreat for the leaders of Grace. She also helped BJ think through new budget issues that were cropping up now that a few families had left Grace Church.

They talked about Bill Harder's leadership of the council and how BJ wished he would take a stronger role in leading Grace in the direction everyone agreed needed to be taken. Through Pam's excellent questions and listening, BJ came to realize that Bill's timid approach might be a blessing because a strong leader as vice president of the council might lead Grace in a different direction. BJ committed to continue to work with Bill on learning to lead with more confidence and courage.

BJ continued to talk regularly with her mom, but now it was mostly to learn what Johanna was up to. As church issues came up, BJ found she was able to bring them to Pam and the four other women in the pastor's network that was taking shape. As their relationships deepened, BJ found she had more clarity about issues and more courage to deal with them.

BJ invited Pam to come and preach at Grace, and Pam did the same with BJ at First. Both were received warmly by the respective congregations. They were fast becoming close friends and gaining a lot of insight and energy from each other's love for serving God by loving their neighbors.

With Pam's coaching BJ was able to clarify in her mind a plan for a vision retreat that would be held in two sessions. She decided to invite all six members of the leadership council and any other interested people from the congregation.

BJ pulled Bill Harder into the planning of the retreat to ensure he felt ownership for it. She also looked for segments he could lead as a way to help him develop as a leader.

BJ invited Charles, Deborah, and Anwar to the retreat, and they all agreed to attend. She also planned to invite Jerome and Chandra, and Ally, who had been faithfully attending the weekly community-church meetings for some time, to come to the second session. She wanted to include them in conversations about how Grace could serve most effectively in its neighborhood, and how it could become a welcoming place for the people who lived there.

Pam and the other network pastors helped BJ think through how she would plan the event in order to achieve three outcomes: 1) a clear statement of mission, 2) a short list of the most closely held values, and 3) a description of what Grace would be doing in five years—a vision of God's future for the church.

Fifteen people attended the first retreat session, which was held in the middle of November. BJ shared with them that they would be discerning God's direction for Grace Church over the coming five years, and that they would be asked to commit to whatever that vision would be. BJ could tell that a couple of people felt nervous about the level of commitment she was expecting, but she was encouraged that they stayed for the entire retreat.

BJ opened the retreat with a devotion on Micah 6:8 and its call for God's people to love mercy, do justice, and walk humbly with God. She wanted to lay a spiritual foundation that would undergird the entire retreat. After the devotion she shared things she had learned were important to any organization, whether professional or voluntary, a business or a church. She explained that every well-run organization needed to be intentional about three key things: its mission or purpose, its values, and its vision.

"Our mission or purpose is the reason we exist in the first place," BJ said. "As a church, our mission has already been

defined by God. Different churches use different words to describe
this mission, but they all express the same thing: that the church
exists to provide people with opportunities to express their love of
God—opportunities to worship, to grow in Christ, and to introduce
others to Jesus Christ by their words and actions."

BJ continued. "Our values are a list of our key behaviors as we
walk together in pursuit of our mission. This list might include
hospitality, creativity, loving relationships, powerful music, great
preaching, strong outreach, vibrant youth ministry, rich senior
ministry, program driven attraction, highly structured worship,
highly informal worship, and so on. During this retreat, let's identify six values we want to be known by as we live out our mission.

"The third thing we need to be intentional about is our vision.
We need to picture the not-too-distant future that God desires for
Grace Church, in other words, an appropriate way to live out our
mission in our context. This is certain to be a destination where
God is already present and where we are being invited to join God.

"I should share with you all that, with regard to a vision of
God's future for Grace Church, over the past few months I've
sensed a tug from God in a particular direction. It's most clearly
captured by the phrase "feed my sheep," which some of you will
recall was the basis for a sermon I gave a few months back. I'm not
at all sure what the particulars of that vision are, and I'm hopeful
that by the end of this retreat they will become more clear."

BJ continued, "Now I'm going to ask Bill Harder to review Grace
Church's mission statement, which the leaders of Grace produced
just prior to my coming on board."

Bill walked to the front of the room and taped up a large poster
with Grace's mission statement written on it:

> Grace Church exists to provide opportunities to praise and
> love God in community, to love our neighbors as ourselves,
> and to make disciples through all the land.

Bill had the participants gather in three groups of four or five
and each answer one of three questions: What does it mean to love
God with all our mind, soul, heart, and strength? What does it

mean to love our neighbors as ourselves? and What does it mean to make disciples?

BJ thought Bill did a great job of leading participants through a challenging dialogue as they explored why Grace Church existed in the first place. Participants who were members of Grace found themselves agreeing that the current mission statement still defined Grace's reasons for doing ministry.

They also realized that they hadn't been living up to this mission for many years—maybe since before any of them could remember. And that it was time to decide if they were finally ready to put God's desires before their personal preferences, treasured traditions, and rooted relationships.

BJ noticed that Charles was very engaged and influential in this portion of the retreat. Over the past months, he had come so far in his understanding of who his neighbors were and how to love them. His speech and actions showed a changed heart, and BJ had come to trust him more and more in his desire and ability to lead.

BJ ended the retreat with an exercise designed to explore which values would be most important to them as they lived out their mission. After time for reflection and listening for the prompting of the Holy Spirit, they listed all of the values that might be considered key to Grace. Then everyone voted to determine the top six values. More than six of the options gained a significant percentage of votes, so they grouped values that were similar or overlapping, prayed again, voted again, and finally produced their list of six values:

Grace – freely receiving it and freely offering it

Hospitality – not just in our hearts but in our behaviors, and especially toward those who may seem different than the majority of people who attend Grace

Authenticity in Relationships – sharing the truth in love and being vulnerable by choosing to trust someone before he or she has earned it

Outreach in the Community – sharing God's good news with those who don't know it

Service in the Community – showing God's love by finding needs in the community that align with one's deepest passions and gifts and then pursuing ways to meet those needs

Obedience to God – willingness to put God's desires and agenda ahead of our personal preferences, treasured traditions, and rooted relationships

They all returned two weeks later to work on developing the vision for Grace Church. This time BJ and the other participants invited Chandra, Jerome, and Ally to attend, too, so a total of eighteen gathered for the second session of the retreat.

To begin, BJ asked Eleanor if she would share what God had been doing in her life. Eleanor told how BJ's sermons had struck a powerful chord inside her. She told everyone about how she had felt on the Sunday when BJ walked her down to the corner store for ice cream—how scared she had been at first and how invigorated she felt afterward.

She told how she came to know that God was calling her to be involved in the neighborhood surrounding Grace Church. How at the time she had wondered why God was calling an old lady like her, but that now she was experiencing God blessing her in ways she would never have dreamed possible. Her life of loneliness and worry had been replaced with one of vibrant new relationships and purpose. The Bible studies with Chandra and Jerome and a few others from the neighborhood meant more to her than she could ever have imagined. Her eyes filled with tears as she spoke and Chandra's did too.

Eleanor said she now had a much better understanding of what Jesus meant when he talked about letting go of your life that you might gain it—and so that you might experience an abundant life.

When Eleanor finished and returned to her seat, BJ sensed it was time for the participants to be silent and listen. She said a short prayer, asking God to speak to their hearts, and asked everyone to simply quiet their minds.

She followed this by asking if anyone in the group had stirrings similar to what Eleanor had experienced. Both Charles and Deborah shared that although they had had some hard conversations about racism and white privilege with the people they were developing relationships with, they also had a deep sense of God's presence and direction. They sensed the Holy Spirit at work, giving them comfort, peace, and joy in spite of the tough times. "I'm excited to get up each morning, wondering what might unfold that day," said Deborah.

BJ asked everyone to reflect on two questions:

- In light of our mission and our values, what might God be calling us to do in our unique context over the next five years that would make the biggest difference for those God loves, both inside and outside the walls of Grace?

- In light of what you've heard people say is stirring in them, what would you think the Holy Spirit is up to in the people of this particular church?

BJ had everyone share their insights, and it was amazing how similar many of them turned out to be.

Throughout the session, Jerome, Chandra, and Ally had added the neighborhood perspective to the discussion, and it proved to be invaluable. It was obvious that their input would save Grace Church from starting down a lot of ministry dead-ends.

Council leader Bill Harder spoke up. "I think I speak for all of us at Grace when I say I can't believe we would ever have succeeded with the one-sided approach we would have taken to ministry in the Heights. Thank you so much, Ally, Jerome, and Chandra, for your willingness to share your insights. It gives us hope that Grace Church really can be a congregation that joins in God's plan for ministry in the Heights."

BJ helped the group sum up the work they had done together in a simple, bold vision for Grace:

- They would honestly seek to make a difference for God in their neighborhood, and especially within four blocks of the church in all directions.

- They would honestly seek to grow as individuals—spiritually, emotionally, and physically—by being more posi-

tive and faith-filled, more intentional about practicing
spiritual disciplines, and more dedicated to eating
healthier and being more active.

- They would use the phrase "Feed My Sheep" as a short-
hand reference to their mission, values, and vision.

The two vision retreat sessions had proven to be powerful for
those who attended. They made plans to communicate what they
had discovered to the rest of the congregation through sermons,
testimonies, and articles in the church newsletter.

Not everyone in the church responded positively to the vision
that had grown out of the retreat. It was easy to see that some folks
wouldn't be around in a year's time. But BJ was excited to see many
people growing in their faith in the direction God was taking them
individually and as a congregation, and acting on that faith. Eleanor
especially continued to grow in courage and as a leader. She began
to take more responsibility for the weekly neighborhood community group that continued to meet in Chandra's living room.

Jerome and Charles teamed up to lead a small gathering just for
men. The men got together to help elderly and financially struggling neighbors maintain their homes. Once a month, a few of the
men gathered for prayer and Bible study as well. One of the men,
Don Fletcher, came to their gathering with an idea that would
prove to be key in reaching out to Grace's neighbors.

Don had read about a city church that sounded a lot like Grace
Church. It was filled with people who drove in from the suburbs
and had no contact with the people who lived near the church,
who were mostly Hispanic. The church started sending letters to
the people who lived near the church, one street at a time. The letters asked if people had any needs that the church could pray for,
and if they did, to send them along to the church.

According to what Don had read, many people from the
church's neighborhood responded, and a group of people at the
church who took these prayer requests very seriously prayed regularly for the needs that came before them. If they had a name and
address, and permission from the person who had turned in the

request to do so, they would follow up to learn more about a particular need and how things were going.

The men's group thought this was a practice Grace Church should adopt. They brought the idea to the council, and the council members agreed. A prayer group formed and sent out the first batch of letters. The response was encouraging: five families and individuals sent prayer requests, and three of these came with permission for follow-up.

People in the Heights really appreciated that people from the church were coming to them instead of expecting the Heights folks to walk through the doors at Grace Church. One woman told a member of the prayer group that she would never have imagined that she would be welcome there.

BJ enthusiastically supported the street-by-street prayer outreach, and she learned about another successful city outreach through her pastors network leader, Pam Dykstra. Pam invited BJ to come experience a ministry to homeless and under resourced people called "5000 Plus" that she and her husband Cal had started a few years earlier. It was located near one of the larger municipal parks in Jefferson City. BJ was encouraged to see how God was using Pam, Cal, and the members of First Church of Jefferson to reach out to people who were struggling in ways that treated them with dignity and respect.[*]

BJ felt like the future of Grace Church was finally taking shape. The vision was clear and well communicated. "Feed My Sheep" was gaining traction. With God's love and guidance, Pam's coaching, her network's encouragement, and her mom's unconditional love, a vibrant, growing church community seemed like more than just a dream.

With things going so well, what happened next caught BJ completely off guard. The most difficult test yet of her courage and commitment was about to come knocking.

---

[*] Learn more about this ministry and the way it took root in *All Things New: A Fable of Renewal*, by Rodger Price. *All Things New* offers a creative way to explore the importance of deep, meaningful relationships in helping Christian leaders grow and become effective in all areas of their lives.

Chapter Fifteen

Deceit and Betrayal

Richard Smit and his youngest son, Jason, had been watching for a way to discredit BJ ever since she'd been called as a pastor of Grace Church. Of course, they didn't think of it that way. They told themselves they were doing what somebody had to do—finding a way to "get their church back." And aside from a few of Richard's closest buddies, no one had a clue what they were up to. Anyone judging by their outward actions and appearances would have described them as upstanding members of Grace Church.

Twenty-eight-year-old Jason worked the night shift at a metal fabrication plant about a mile from the church. For the past year, Richard had used him to track which nights BJ's car was in her driveway. He wanted to prove his suspicion that she was "shacking up with that boyfriend of hers."

Depending on how busy the plant was, Jason got off work between one and four in the morning. On his drive home, he would drive slowly past the parsonage and record the date and time if it appeared that BJ wasn't home.

Richard realized he needed more than Jason's log to bring to the elders. He wanted to go beyond taking the wind out of BJ's sails. It was his goal to entirely discredit her. He fantasized about BJ leaving in disgrace, never to lead another church, ever.

One afternoon before heading to work, Jason reported to Richard that BJ's boyfriend had been at the parsonage at three in the morning. He'd seen the boyfriend's car when he had driven by the parsonage on his way home the night before. He recognized the car as the same one he and Richard had seen the man driving when he'd picked BJ up after worship one Sunday last July.

Richard smiled. This was the break he'd been looking for, a chance to get the kind of evidence he needed. He loaned Jason his digital camera, and over the next few weeks Jason photographed Michael's car in the driveway twice between two and three in the morning. Jason reported that no lights had been on inside the house, which he also had photographed. The camera conveniently dated and time-stamped each photo.

Richard printed the photos and carefully stored the memory card that held the images. It was time to approach Bill Harder, the head of the leadership council, and let him know what kind of a pastor Grace really had.

After the Sunday service just two weeks before Easter, Richard followed Bill Harder out into the parking lot. Richard knew the leadership council was scheduled to meet the next evening. It was time to drag BJ's dirty laundry out in the open.

"Bill!" Richard called. Bill turned and waited for Richard. "Bill, I have something special to bring to the leadership council tomorrow night."

"Oh, really? What's it about?"

"I guess you could say it's about the future of Grace Church." He kept his face open and friendly. He wanted Bill to assume he would be delivering good news.

"I'm all ears," said Bill, and he waited for Richard to continue.

Richard said, "It's really something I've spent a lot of time on. Something I'd like to present to the whole council myself. Do you have, say, ten minutes on the agenda when I could do that?"

"I think I could arrange that. We start at seven-thirty. I usually meet with BJ in her office at seven to pray and go over things before the meeting. Why don't you join us? That way we'll have an idea of what you want to present."

Richard wasn't crazy about the way this was going, but he couldn't see a way to back out now. He spotted Jason standing across the parking lot beside their car watching them. "Sure, that'll be fine. See you tomorrow, Bill," he said. He walked over to Jason.

"Dad, what's up?"

"I just got on the council agenda for tomorrow's meeting. I'd say it's about time they faced the truth about BJ."

"Dad, are you sure you want to go ahead with this? I mean, the more I look at it, I'm not sure we can really prove anything."

Richard shot Jason a look of disdain. "You, too? You're defending that woman! I ask you, what else would those two be up to at that time of the night? Hmmm...middle of the night, man and a woman, no lights on." He yelled, "Do I have to draw you a freaking picture?"

A few people who were walking toward their cars turned and stared. Richard angrily motioned Jason to get in the car. He revved the engine, slammed it in gear, and sped out of the lot. He didn't say one word to Jason that entire afternoon.

* * * * *

Just before seven on Monday evening, Richard pulled into the church parking lot. Bill's car was already there. As he entered the church, Richard heard Bill's and BJ's voices and walked down the hall toward BJ's office.

As he stepped through the doorway, BJ turned to greet him. She was startled by the anger in Richard's eyes. She was about to ask what was the matter when he blurted out, "Barbara, I know you're wondering why I'm here, and I would like to get right to it."

"Okay. Why don't you have a seat?"

Bill didn't seem to know what to think. He stared at Richard.

"Richard," he said, "What the heck is this about?"

Richard ignored him and spoke directly to BJ, his eyes narrowing. "I know that you are living in sin. I demand that you come clean and tell the entire council what has been going on with you and the man you've been 'dating.' I guess that's what it's called now."

BJ frowned at Richard. "Richard, I don't have the faintest idea what you're talking about."

Richard turned to Bill. His voice grew louder. "She's been entertaining a certain man at all hours at her house, or should I say *our* house. I have photos, and they don't lie!"

Richard took a step toward BJ. "I think you know what I'm talking about all right. In plain English, you are having an inappropriate relationship with a man who is not your husband!"

BJ felt like she had dropped down the rabbit hole in *Alice in Wonderland*. "How in the world could you have any idea what is going on between me and Michael?"

Richard ignored her. "Bill and I will be sharing this with the leadership council first thing tonight. I suggest you have your head together by then and decide what you want to say."

BJ replied evenly. "I have done absolutely nothing to be ashamed of, Richard. It's obvious that you *think* you know something, and I'll be as interested as anyone to hear what it is."

BJ's calmness surprised Richard and it even surprised her. Her experiences over the past year had changed BJ in some fundamental way. Whatever she faced this evening, she knew God would not abandon her or Grace Church.

BJ asked Bill and Richard to leave so she could pray before the meeting. Bill left looking confused and upset. Richard stomped down the hall toward the men's room. BJ thought about calling Pam, but there wasn't enough time. She called on God for guidance and strength instead.

BJ felt the calm that came over her whenever she was especially aware of the presence of the Holy Spirit. She had a clear sense that there was nothing to fear. She recalled how often scripture says "fear not" and the passage in Romans 8: "If God is for us, who is against us?" Trust and depend on God. That is what she would do.

BJ walked into the room just before the council meeting started. Bill glanced her way as she sat down and turned to face the council. "Before we dive into our agenda, Richard Smit has something he wants to share with us," she said. BJ stared directly at Bill and then at Richard in a way that communicated to the group that she was aware of what was about to be shared.

Richard stood to address the group. "I'll get right to the point. I have evidence that our spiritual leader, Pastor Barbara, has been having an inappropriate relationship with a man to whom she is not married. I'm here to bring this totally unacceptable behavior to your attention." He looked right at BJ. She held his gaze and remained silent. No one spoke. For a few moments the room was so quiet that anyone standing in the hallway would have assumed it was empty.

Richard sat down and began again. "After you learn more about what has taken place, I suggest that either she explains this sinful life-choice to the congregation next Sunday and publicly repents, or that she offers her resignation to us by Wednesday so we have time to find someone to preach in her place this Sunday."

All eyes were on BJ to see how she would respond. BJ took her time, looking each of them in the eyes before speaking. "Well, I have to share with you, my friends, my leaders, my flock, that I just learned of these accusations minutes ago. I also have to tell you that I am shocked at how this accusation is being communicated."

Bill looked sheepish and Eleanor seemed agitated.

BJ continued. "Let me process some thoughts out loud with you. After hearing this from Richard about a half-hour ago I am left wondering what Richard thinks he knows and just as importantly how he came to know it."

Richard jumped up and slammed his open palm down on the table. "What I've come to know is that you're sleeping with that friend of yours. And I have photos to prove it." He threw his stack of parsonage photos on the table, and was about to begin explaining what they proved.

BJ cut him off. "Richard, with all due respect, in fact with more respect than is due, let me speak!" She continued, calmly and with authority. "I wonder how an accusation like this would be handled if I were an older white man? I wonder if this would be handled differently if we weren't making difficult changes in Grace's ministry that you might not be all that pleased with. I wonder if this is a set-up just to stop us from moving forward in the vision that God has placed on our hearts for Grace.

"Richard, please explain this so-called evidence of what you think I have done."

Richard hesitated. BJ's calm demeanor had planted a seed of doubt that he was on solid ground. His voice trembled a bit and he spoke more quietly. "I know that you have been spending entire nights with a man you aren't married to. I know this has happened several times at our parsonage. This is fornication, which is clearly sin. Our spiritual leader should not be living a life of sin and then preach to us about her 'social justice' message."

BJ asked, "Richard, where did you get these photos?"

He didn't skip a beat. "My son works third shift at a factory near here, and he has seen this man's car in the driveway several times when he's driven by late at night. He has also noticed many times when your car was not in the driveway at all."

BJ calmly said, "Richard, would it be fair to say that you have had your son spying on me?"

"I know what I know, and that you should resign here and now!" Richard snapped. He abruptly sat down, folded his arms, and waited for BJ to respond.

BJ didn't speak right away. Then, just as Bill looked ready to say something, she jumped in ahead of him.

"Everything I know says not to dignify this very inappropriate attack with a response. However, I love all of you, and Grace Church, and God most of all."

Bill poured BJ a glass of water, and she took a sip before continuing. "It might be tempting to offer my resignation, because no one deserves to be treated this way."

She paused again. She wanted to choose her words carefully. "It would be interesting to know what might come to light about all of our lives if people were assigned to spy on each of us. Who among us is without sin? And I'm not saying that I have sinned, but even if I had, would I deserve to be stoned in public like Richard is trying to do?"

Richard looked like he was going to speak again, and BJ held up her hand to stop him.

"God has given me a mission, and I refuse to give in to this attack and risk the good thing that God is doing here at Grace and will do in the future. So I will respond.

"I have had a serious relationship with a man named Michael Sheldon for almost a year now. I have kept it quiet because the fishbowl-life of a single female pastor is not a good incubator for a new relationship. Michael and I have fallen deeply in love over the past year, and we have decided to get married. We had planned to do this quietly back in my hometown and announce it to all of you after the ceremony.

Richard shifted uncomfortably in his seat.

BJ said, "Of late Michael and I have been spending late evenings together. We have a lot to plan and talk about. So Richard, while the 'intelligence' your spy has provided is accurate, it is in no way proof of what you claim has taken place between me and Michael."

There was another long uncomfortable pause before she continued. "But you should know this about your spiritual leader. Christ is my master. I will not walk away from him. I believe I am okay with him. But as I often do, I will search my heart for any sin and repent of it. If I need to confess to another person or persons, I will do this with the pastors in my network and with my coach, Pastor Pam. I will share with them all that has happened here tonight. They already know about Michael and our relationship. Please know that I will be as honest as I know how to be with myself, with God, with my coach, and with the members of my pastors group. If they suggest I have something to confess to all of you, I promise you I will do that.

"As I commit to search my soul, I ask each of you to do the same.

"I will not offer my resignation now, nor will I offer it by Wednesday, unless you decide not to reprimand Richard for the way he has worked in the shadows, looking for a way to undermine me and Grace Church. He has tried to undermine the mission and vision God has laid on the hearts of the leaders of Grace. And he has used grossly inappropriate ways to bring his accusations to this body.

"Members of the council, please don't pretend this didn't happen. This must be addressed." She paused and looked at each person at the table in turn.

"I will leave now so that you can decide what to do. I am going to pray for you, for your deliberations, for Grace Church, and for Richard, too."

BJ rose and walked to the door. She stepped into the hall and closed the door softly but firmly behind her.

BJ slipped through the side door in her office and half-walked half-ran across the church parking lot to the parsonage. Home. A bit of refuge. Her front door stood open on this warm, still April evening. BJ stumbled and almost fell as she yanked the screen door open and stepped inside. Tears started to flow along with prayers as she sank to her couch.

Would God allow all the progress of the last six months to be wiped away in a single stroke? Just when it looked like months of fighting the good fight were beginning to pay off. Her heart ached when she thought of Grace's chance for renewed ministry slipping away.

God's call had been clear: "Feed my sheep!" Her mind drifted over the series of events that had rocked Grace Church and its neighborhood over the past year.

BJ's time serving Grace Church had been a patchwork of storm and sunshine. At times ministry had gotten so tough that BJ asked herself how in the world she had come to this place. People she had thought were her friends had turned away from her. "God, where are you in all of this?" BJ cried.

After a while she seemed to run out of tears and just sat quietly. She glanced at the clock on the table beside her. It was after nine. Pale light from a streetlamp fell across the floor, and a passing car's heavy bass vibrated the floorboards beneath her feet. She pulled herself up to close and bolt the front door, dragged herself upstairs, and crawled into bed. The bed he'd accused her of sharing with Michael!

She wanted to sleep, but her mind wouldn't shut down. She thought she heard a muffled roll of thunder in the distance. *Well, bring it on*, she thought. *I'm ready for a storm!*

A flash of lightning lit the room and a crack of thunder shook the window panes. Rain began a steady patter on the roof. It was a sound that always soothed BJ, and she drifted off.

Chapter Sixteen

An Emerging Leader

After BJ left the council meeting, everyone had looked around wondering what to say and do next. Richard rose to leave. "I think I've said everything I needed to say. Now it's up to you."

Before he reached the door, Eleanor surprised everyone by standing so abruptly that her chair tipped over. "Richard, wait a minute. I need to share what's on my mind with you."

"No, I don't think I need to stay for that."

Bill spoke up. "I insist that you listen to what Eleanor has to say. This is a very serious matter. Others may want to speak as well."

Richard scowled, but he stayed, standing just inside the door. Eleanor looked Richard in the eye. Her voice shook with anger.

"Why would you do this evil thing? I am disgusted by your actions. Pastor Barbara is the best thing that has happened to Grace Church in more than twenty years. I will fight you to the end if you think you are going to drive her away from us."

She turned to the others. "I submit that Richard be disciplined for his actions. And if he doesn't accept that discipline, we need to ask him to leave Grace Church."

Richard looked around for support and momentarily took comfort when he saw Bill preparing to speak. But what Bill had to say shocked him.

"I'm embarrassed that I was any part of this. When I invited Richard to meet with Pastor Barbara just prior to coming to our meeting, I was under the impression he had some positive news that he wanted to deliver to the council in person. Now I have to say that I agree with Eleanor. Richard, this is a terrible thing you have done. What you're trying to do would destroy not only BJ but this entire congregation."

Richard looked like he'd been punched in the gut. No one was going to come to his aid. Their expressions and silence told him all he needed to know: they agreed with Eleanor and Bill.

Bill spoke again. "Richard, please leave. We need to discuss what your appropriate discipline will be."

Richard's face reddened. "This is a sad day in the history of what used to be Grace Church—our Grace Church!" he yelled. Richard stormed out of the room, slamming the door behind him. His footsteps echoed in the hallway and another door slammed as he left the building.

Eleanor again was first to speak. "Let's take a break. I'll walk over to BJ's to tell her what has just happened. She needs to know right away that we support her."

Eleanor opened the side door of the church only to discover that a storm was moving in. The wind was picking up and a few big raindrops hit her face and spotted her dress. She glanced over at BJ's. All the lights were out. She took her phone from her purse and called BJ's number. When her voicemail picked it up, Eleanor left a short message. "Pastor, this is Eleanor. The meeting ended on a very positive note. Everything will be fine. I'll tell you all about it first thing in the morning."

When she returned to the meeting room, Eleanor explained that BJ was apparently in bed and that she planned to contact her right away the next day. Bill suggested they call it a night and the others agreed. It had been one council meeting none of them would ever forget.

* * * * *

The next morning Eleanor was up with the sun and so eager to tell BJ what had taken place that she hopped in her car right after breakfast. She had already left BJ another message telling her she was on her way, that she wanted to talk face to face.

As Eleanor stepped up the walk to BJ's house, drops of rain sparkled on leaves and grass like countless gems. The breeze shook a few drops down on Eleanor. Green shoots were beginning to poke through the black earth next to BJ's porch. Her front door stood open a crack, and Eleanor called, "Yoo-hoo!" and stepped inside.

"Eleanor, welcome!" BJ called from the kitchen. "I listened to your messages this morning. Come join me for a cup of coffee."

Sitting across the kitchen table from BJ, Eleanor described what had happened after BJ had left the council meeting the night before. "I guess I was almost as surprised as Richard when I took him on in front of the whole group," she said. "Bill Harder called me this morning. He says the council needs to meet again, this week if possible, to figure out how to discipline Richard. Bill says to tell you he hopes you'll join us for the discussion."

Later that morning, Eleanor and BJ parted with a long hug. Eleanor was on her way to Chandra's house to talk about planning summer activities for the members of the community study group. BJ stood at her front door and watched Eleanor get in her car and wave goodbye. She closed her eyes and inhaled the scent of rain-washed air. She would get a run in before going to the office. Praise God! Life was back on track.

* * * * *

The council met again that Wednesday evening. When BJ walked in, council members took turns assuring her that they were behind her. A member made a motion to discipline Richard and another seconded it. There was no discussion or debate. The council voted unanimously to take the strongest disciplinary measures available short of removing Richard's membership at Grace Church.

Bill again apologized to the council and to BJ in particular for how he had handled things. "I should have confronted Richard, like Eleanor did," he said. "Eleanor, I admire your spunk!" Bill added that he would contact Richard and let him know what they had decided.

They took time to pray—for BJ, for themselves, for Grace Church, and for the people of Jefferson Heights. They also prayed for Richard and Jason. They were filled with peace about where things stood and what needed to be done.

* * * * *

In the end, the test of commitment Richard brought to BJ and Grace Community was a catalyst for the congregation's revitalization. At the next council meeting, Bill gave a short devotional on

Romans 8:28: "We know that all things work together for good for those who love God, who are called according to his purpose." He spoke about how God had clearly used a set of events orchestrated by dark powers to strengthen and embolden the leaders of Grace Church. The mission and vision that God had given them was being lived out more powerfully than ever.

Bill also informed the council that when he had approached Richard with the council's plan for his discipline, he had reacted with anger. Richard had told Bill he would remove his and Jason's membership from Grace Church. Jason had called a few days later to say he disagreed with his dad's decision and wanted to retain his membership. The council agreed to this, on the condition that Jason meet with BJ and Bill Harder as soon as possible.

When Richard left, he took two families that had been longtime members with him. They had been listening to his dark pro-nouncements on BJ's fitness for ministry for some time. His version of the events the night of the council meeting had convinced them that Grace Church was no longer "their" church. Over the years the significant financial gifts these families had made had provided as much as 15 percent of the church's overall budget, al-though recently they had given significantly less.

While their departures created a financial challenge for the church, not one person on the council expressed any doubt that Grace Church would continue its ministry. Several people, including Deborah, Charles, and Eleanor, tripled their giving commit-ment for the coming year. Two of the pastors in BJ's network convinced their churches to provide Grace Church with a twelve-month pledge of support to help them make ends meet.

Whenever BJ reflected on the events of the past couple of years she was amazed and filled with gratitude. It was humbling to see how God's hand was evident every step of the way. The tune to the doxology would pop into BJ's head and she would find herself singing: "Praise God, from whom all blessings flow..."

Chapter Seventeen

Grace I Give to You

Now that what would prove to be BJ's biggest battle was behind her, she found herself looking forward with excitement. Everywhere BJ could see signs that new life had been breathed into ministry in the congregation and the community.

More people in the congregation were demonstrating that they were growing in faith as they stepped up to serve inside and outside the walls of Grace Church. Many took a class to help them identify their spiritual gifts and then found ways to practice them. Several older members began working with a local elementary school to begin planning an after-school mentoring program for kids who were struggling socially and academically. The halls of the church building now echoed with footsteps, conversation, and laughter just as they had years ago.

One week that summer, Charles and Deborah asked BJ to meet them for lunch at Ally's Place. She thought maybe something was wrong, but it turned out that they just wanted to buy her lunch and share how God was moving in their lives. They thanked BJ for all that she had done for them and was doing for the church.

BJ was still helping with devotionals for the evening community study group that Chandra and Eleanor led together. Ally and a few other friends from the Heights were regulars too. Every so often, a couple of the members of the group would attend Sunday worship at Grace Church, and they were warmly welcomed when they did.

Anwar had become a regular attendee at Grace Church, and he'd asked to meet with BJ to discuss membership. Once in a while Anwar's sister, Yasmin, and her husband, Aamir, came with Anwar to worship. BJ visited their restaurant at least once a month and discovered that she loved the spicy hot Pakistani dishes they offered.

God moved Charles and Deborah to invest in the Heights neighborhood in a very literal sense. They decided to buy a neighborhood home that was in disrepair and fix it up. They said it was a new version of their dream of a "cottage by the lake"—it was located on a kind of spiritual lake, a place where they could be renewed by helping others, where they could live a life of mission.

Once Charles and Deborah began spending weekends at their urban cottage, Charles started a ministry called The Carpenter's Tools. He invited friends in the neighborhood and Grace members to donate tools to be loaned one Saturday a month to anyone in the neighborhood who needed them. He also encouraged Grace members to help the tool "renter" with the work he or she needed to do. Sometimes tool renters made a donation to the ministry when they borrowed a tool, but none was required.

Jerome knew home repair better than anyone Charles had ever met, and he was a huge help with the tool ministry. Jerome usually went along with a member of Grace to help with projects in neighborhood homes. With his supervision, projects tended to go a lot smoother and a lot faster.

All in all, the tools program was a great way to show people in the community that members of Grace Church really cared about them. Sometimes misunderstandings arose between community folks and church folks. But with God's grace and a willingness to work things out, most could be resolved.

Several neighbors who benefitted from The Carpenter's Tools ministry checked out a worship service or two. Unfortunately they didn't quite feel at home with the congregation and the worship style. Over time BJ and others were working on ways to address this, including taking a thoughtful approach to hospitality for visitors.

BJ and Michael quietly got married in BJ's hometown of Murietta, Georgia, attended by her family, old friends, and several new friends: Eleanor, Charles, Deborah, Chandra, and Jerome, and Pam and the other members of the pastors network. The folks from Jefferson Heights all rented a bus together for the ride down to Murrieta.

Michael began to regularly attend Sunday services at Grace

Church but mostly kept his distance from BJ's "professional world." Along with BJ's pastors network and her coach, Pam, Michael provided a safe place where BJ could be fully known and loved.

Over time Chandra and Jerome started to attend Sunday worship services and form friendships with a few people in the church. At first Grace members tended to be awkward around them, not sure about how to act or what to say. BJ gave Chandra and Jerome a lot of credit for hanging in there and for being gracious when someone would try too hard to be pleasant or unintentionally say something offensive. With God's grace and people's willingness to pursue the vision God had placed on their hearts, true relationships were beginning to replace polite chatter.

Grace Church was once again living up to its name—it was becoming a place of love and acceptance for all. And BJ still served up a tough message from time to time, as always, seasoned with love and grace.

What Happened Next?

As the years rolled by at Grace Church in Jefferson Heights, BJ, Michael, Eleanor, Chandra, Jerome, Anwar, Yasmin, and Deborah and Charles developed deeper relationships than they could ever have imagined they would a few years earlier.

Feed My Sheep continues to be the "bumper sticker" version of Grace's mission, values, and vision. Everyone knows what the words stand for and most are actively involved in living out the vision it describes. And even though Jesus didn't mean for his words to be taken literally when he told Peter, "Feed my sheep," food has come to play a central role in Grace's ministry.

BJ, Michael, Eleanor, and Chandra throw simple dinner parties for neighbors on the fourth Saturday of each month. These parties seem to break down many of the walls that have been built over the years between the neighbors and Grace Church members. "Breaking bread" together is a powerful way to build community. It's hard to judge someone that you enjoy food and conversation with.

In the summertime, Charles and Deborah began holding similar gatherings at their new "cottage." On a designated evening, about two dozen people from the neighborhood and a dozen members of Grace Church gather to share food and fun.

With the help of Eleanor and a couple of men in the congregation, Chandra has started a community garden on a plot of land donated for that purpose by the city of Jefferson Heights. She put up a sign with her phone number that said, "Help with this garden and share in the harvest." Not many people turned out to help the first year, and at first a lot of the ripe veggies mysteriously disappeared overnight. But when the Jefferson Heights police department started having officers patrol neighborhoods on bikes, the veggie theft fell off dramatically. The second year more people were encouraged to garden, the size of the garden grew, and now dozens of people share cucumbers, tomatoes, beans, and carrots. Eleanor cans anything that's left over and invites neighbors to the church kitchen to learn how.

When word began to spread about the garden, how good the fresh food was, and how much canned food made it into people's homes, it created a lot of buzz in the community. So when Chandra distributed flyers announcing that she would teach residents how to start their own gardens, and that Charles and his Carpenter's Tools rental gang would help till the soil, six people decided to plant their own gardens in the coming spring.

Over several years the neighborhood's overall appearance began to reflect all the hard work people had been doing, with nicely painted homes, neat lawns, and gardens. And more and more neighbors began to attend all kinds of church functions like Bible studies and classes that taught people how to track their expenses, apply for financial aid for college, or do their own taxes. While there continue to be real challenges for the future of Grace Church, for the first time in many years it seems like there is hope for the future—a future clearly tied to Jesus' call to Peter to "feed my sheep."

Eventually Grace Church formed a 501(c)(3), or non-profit. Donors funded the garden project and the tool rental program and expanded them in a way that created one full-time and one part-time job for two people from the neighborhood. The goal of the non-profit is to build the community by building the people in it. When the local news station told the fledgling organization's story, the mayor decided to get behind it. Now the whole city is learning about Grace's mission, values, and vision.

BJ and Michael are expecting a baby, and beginning a whole new chapter of their life together. It's bound to be challenging for BJ to lead Grace Church and be a mom, but the people who know her best aren't too concerned. They know BJ loves a challenge.

Exploring the Leadership Principles in *Grace in the Heights*

I hope you enjoyed the story of Grace Church and Pastor BJ. I enjoyed working with editor Ann Saigeon to develop a story that would allow me to share leadership principles that I have found to be helpful in my own journey and in my leadership development consulting.

Together we tried to write a fictional story that would integrate many of the issues pastors face and include realistic examples of how a pastor can proactively and responsively deal with the challenge of leading a congregation through significant change.

While I think that Grace Church's journey might be a particularly challenging one, I believe it is representative of what many mainline denominational churches experience today.

Following is a description of eight leadership principles that I wove into the story. I'm identifying and describing them in some detail here, with the hope that readers will consider applying these principles in their own contexts.

1. Transformation in an organization is almost always preceded by transformation in its leader or a group of its leaders.

In the Reformed Church in America, where I work primarily with pastors, we have an often-used saying: "Personal transformation precedes congregational transformation, which precedes gospel impact in the world."

In the case of Grace Church, a move toward change came with a new leader, Pastor Barbara, who was a very different kind of leader than the one the congregation had previously. Grace Church's move toward transformation gathered momentum once key leaders in the church took a hard look their current reality and embraced the need for deep change.

An existing leader also can spark new life in a congregation. This happens when a significant event or experience changes the leader's approach to life, to the organization he or she leads, or to leadership itself. An example of this kind of personal transformation can be found in another fable I wrote called *All Things New: A Fable of Renewal*. It can be downloaded free at www.all-things-new.org.

Regardless of how new life springs up in an organization, whether through existing leaders or through the recruitment of a new leader, one thing remains clear: "You will continue to get what you've got if you continue to do what you've done." Living Systems Theory puts it this way: "The results you are getting are exactly what your system is set up to give you." Something has to change if you are going to experience a future other than the one you're headed toward.

2. Prayer is crucial to the transformation of a church (or a person).

I'm not sure if I put enough prayer in the story of Grace Church. BJ's life and the life of the congregation are radically dependent on prayer. In fact, prayer is often what sparks transformation deep in a leader's core being.

Ultimately, the transformation of a church is God's doing. God allows us to join in the fun, so to speak, and it starts with prayer—with asking God to change us individually and collectively. Many churches don't do much of this. Pastors and churches that have gone through deep transformational change consistently tell me that they did a lot of praying. Some pastors have told me that praying was the only really intentional thing they did at the beginning of a change that brought new life.

Should we be surprised by this? I don't think we should. When Jesus taught his disciples about the impending harvest he began by saying, "The harvest truly is great, but the laborers are few; therefore pray the Lord of the harvest to send out laborers into His harvest" (Luke 10:2, NKJV). He didn't tell the disciples to get out there and start harvesting; he told them to start with prayer.

I'm not an expert on prayer, so I won't try to describe how you might go about it in your congregation. I will, however, suggest you read chapter four, "The Power of Prayer," from the book *The U-Turn Church: New Direction for Health and Growth*, by Kevin Harney and Bob Bouwer. It is an easy read and gives good suggestions for how prayer can be transformed in your congregation so that your congregation might be transformed by prayer.

3. The transformation path of an organization will include landmines.

It's been said that the only person who wants a change is a baby. OK, that's a bit of an exaggeration, but it's true that many people dislike change and will naturally resist it. There are a lot of theories about why this is the case, and maybe I'll write about that in another fable.

Bobby Kennedy has been quoted as saying, "Twenty percent of the people will be against anything." I can imagine some of you saying, "Amen!"

Because change is difficult for many people, and because some people will truly be against the transformed beliefs and values that are driving the change, a leader can expect that some very anxious people will speak up. I love author and counselor Trisha Taylor's expression: "Anxiety makes me stupid." And it isn't just Trisha who gets stupid when she's anxious. We all do unless we have developed ways to manage our anxiety and our thinking.

A wise leader knows that she will face some good people acting stupidly in the midst of change and anxiety. The leader knows it's important to have skills and strategies that will help her get beyond the irrational arguments that often arise from anxious people. BJ's strategy was to speak with her mother, Johanna, and later her coach, Pam, before engaging the anxious person. Both women brought a non-anxious presence to BJ that helped her regain a clear mind and remember who she was, what she believed, and how she could best handle the difficulty in front of her.

Of course a leader won't always be able to take time to reflect before responding to the "stupidity" of an anxious person. That makes it tougher to respond productively, but even something as simple as counting to ten before responding can allow a leader's brain to move from an anxious/non-thinking state to a less-anxious/more-thinking state. And doing so can pay huge dividends.

4. The transformation of a church takes a long time.

Most experts on the subject say the transformation or revitalization of a church takes seven to ten or even fifteen years— a long time!

I am reminded of the description of the Stockdale Paradox in Jim Collins's book *Good to Great: Why Some Companies Make the Leap...and Others Don't*. The paradox is named after Vice Admiral James Stockdale. As a prisoner of war in Vietnam, Stockdale was able to do two very difficult things that seem paradoxical: deal honestly with the brutal facts and never lose faith in the outcome. Stockdale learned that the prisoners of war who coped best were the ones who dealt honestly with the brutal facts of their situation while never losing faith that one day they would be released.

Pastors whom I have interviewed regarding the turn-around of a church they were leading have talked about the early days of the transformation and the very difficult, even brutal facts they had to deal with. I clearly caught a sense in them, however, that they didn't question whether they were doing the right thing. They persisted when others might not have, and they were rewarded by seeing the fruits of their labors, but not before they had been at it for a long time.

Romans 5 says to rejoice in our sufferings because "suffering produces endurance, and endurance produces character, and character produces hope, and hope does not disappoint us, because God's love has been poured into our hearts through the Holy Spirit that has been given to us." Maybe Jim Collins should have just quoted scripture to get his point across.

The story of Grace Church presents a pretty quick turn-around. Of course BJ is an amazing leader, which would help things go better and faster than in a situation where the leader is not as developed. She also did something that I suspect

most leaders would never do: BJ insisted that Richard be dealt
with appropriately after his diabolical attempt to undermine
her. She demanded that he be disciplined in line with the
policies and polity of the church. While churches of virtually
all denominations have policies and polity in place for this
purpose, I suspect they are rarely used, even when it's
appropriate.

One pastor told me that the successful turn-around of the
church he led could have happened a lot sooner if he would
have been willing to take disciplinary measures sooner rather
than later in the process. He told me that this is the one thing
he would do differently if he were to do it all over again.

5. Leaders of transformation must establish clear mission, values, and vision.

Highly effective leaders know that clarity of vision begins
with them. BJ was clear about who she was and what God was
calling her to do long before she showed up at Grace. She was
clear from an early age about how a church should be, and
this clarity made a big difference in her courage and faith
regarding what needed to be done.

In the fable *All Things New* (download it free at www.all-
things-new.org), Pastor Cal was not so clear about who he
was and what God was calling him to do. In the story, Tony,
another pastor, invites Cal to join a small group of pastors for
an intentional process of gaining clarity around three things:

• God's purpose for his life.
• Beliefs and values God had been forming in him.
• What God was calling him to do with his life.

In *Grace in the Heights*, BJ goes beyond her personal vision
and works to establish a collective vision for Grace. This
process begins with a revelation she has that is associated
with the phrase "feed my sheep." Through the Holy Spirit she
gains clarity about God's purpose for Grace Church, and she

then brings other congregational leaders into a vision discernment process that leads them to embrace the vision as their own.

Leadership author and former Herman Miller CEO Max DePree has said, "A leader's first job is to define reality." I would add that defining reality includes saying what is so today and what needs to be so in God's preferred future. BJ does this by engaging the leaders of Grace around the three key components of any organization's identity:

1. <u>Mission or Purpose</u>: Mission describes the reason an organization exists in the first place. God gave all churches pretty much the same reason to exist: to love and praise God, to love each other, and to make disciples of all people. However, each church needs to figure this out for itself and then state it in a way that speaks clearly to them.

2. <u>Values</u>: Values spell out the highest priorities for how a particular organization goes about doing its work. Like mission, most Christian values are pretty much the same for all churches. However, the list is so long that these values need to be prioritized for each specific church, and this is where churches can have significant differences. For instance, all churches value hospitality, but some make it one of their top values. No church is against creativity, but some make it very easy to see that it is a top value. Music is important to almost all churches, and yet some would name it as one of the most important aspects of their ministry.

Churches that can clearly identify their top values give people who visit a strong sense of whether the congregation would be a good fit for them. A church where members aren't clear about their values as a congregation can give visitors (and members!) a confused idea of what the priorities are.

Great momentum is gained when a congregation's values
are clearly understood by all and lived out with courage
and faithfulness.

3. Vision: Vision is a picture of what a church is working to
   achieve over the coming months or years. Vision describes the best way a church can live out its mission and
   values in its current context.

   God's purpose for a church is clear: to love and praise
   God, love others, and make disciples. All churches exist
   to do these things, but they might pursue them in different ways. This is where clear vision comes in. One
   church might focus on showing God's love to teachers
   and children in the elementary school down the block,
   while another may choose to focus on helping substance
   abusers, addicts, and prostitutes find their way to God.
   Yet another may focus on providing the best Bible study
   opportunities in the area so that God's Spirit and grace
   work through the Word in individual lives.

   Whatever the vision is, it should give a particular church
   the best chance to live out its mission and values in its
   current reality.

Ultimately, BJ and the leaders of Grace Church came to
know that they existed to make a difference in their neighborhood. They came to realize that this wasn't just for the good of
the people in Jefferson Heights, but for their own good as well.
Eleanor experienced this when she found joy and fulfillment
as she sought to reach beyond her self-imposed limitations
and trust God to bring her into meaningful relationships with
people in the Heights.

God desires this abundant life for all of us. But first we have
to let go of our deeply held desires and latch on to God's desires. We're told by Jesus that when we put him ahead of our

personal preferences, treasured traditions, and rooted relationships we will experience a different way of living, a more
abundant way of living.

6. Leaders of transformation are intentional about building a team.

While BJ didn't have a staff, she was still intentional about
building a team. She was on the lookout for people that God
might call to be part of Grace's mission. This happened with
Eleanor, Trina, Jerome, Bill, and Chandra to name a few.

Effective leaders keep their eyes and ears open to discover
who might be used by God in the stated mission. And often
God surprises leaders with who gets stirred up by the Holy
Spirit.

Eleanor was a surprise to me when I was writing. I was
deep into the story, intent on writing about BJ's sermon and
all of a sudden in my mind here was this older woman that
God was stirring up as she sat in the pew. This is one of my favorite parts of the story. It shows that when you're doing what
God is doing, you will get blessed in surprising ways. When
you're doing what you want to do and just asking God to bless
it, there likely won't be any surprise blessings.

God also stirred up Charles and Deborah. They went from
being supportive, to being disgruntled with BJ, to buying all
the way into Grace's mission and actually moving to live in
the neighborhood that surrounded the church. I know of several cases where these kinds of things have actually happened. God stirs people to become what God desires. A leader
just needs to be open to identifying where that might be happening.

I know of churches that provide formal training and re-
sources to help people identify their gifts and passions so that
they can aligned them with their church's or community's
greatest needs. BJ didn't do that formally but you can see how

she tapped into Eleanor's stirrings to make a difference in the neighborhood, and how she started to tap into Trina's gift for cooking, Chandra's gift for working with the earth, and Jerome's gifts for organizing and outreach.

God has gifted each of us uniquely and aligned several of these gifts with our passions. I believe a leader like BJ needs to keep eyes and ears open to sense when a person's gifts and passions intersect with the needs of people God desires to help.

BJ also developed her ministry team by investing in Bill Harder, who may or may not have been well aligned for the leadership role he was in. Because he was in that role, BJ purposefully tried to help him grow. For example, she had him take a significant role in the mission, values, and vision discernment retreat. Not only did he lead portions of the retreat well, he did it better than she thought he might. Again, I've seen this happen in real life many times. Both the leader who challenges someone and the one who steps up are surprised by how well things turn out.

7. With transformation, there will be blood!

Transition can be a time of violent conflict. I've heard of more than one pastor who was leading a congregation in transition and whose life had been threatened by a church member. You may think I'm exaggerating, but I wouldn't kid around about something so serious.

There will be significant conflict in a church revitalization journey. For that reason I've come to believe that it's critical that church leaders be willing and able to engage people who disagree with them in healthy ways.

Avoiding difficult discussions and decisions causes relationships and ministries to become impotent. In attempting to avoid difficult discussions we increase the likelihood that we will experience highly toxic levels of conflict that can and will destroy the church.

BJ handled conflicts in pretty much the same way, regardless of how each arose. In each case she worked to be as non-anxious as possible, she sought to gain full understanding of the other person, and then she sought to be understood. I tried to represent her as realistically as possible even though she handled conflict much better than most of us would.

I have used this model in real life situations about fifty times—not always as well as BJ does, but sometimes pretty close. I have found that virtually every time it has made a situation better and it almost always strengthens relationships, just like it did for BJ, Charles, and Deborah.

The conflict model I describe in the story is one I cobbled together from various sources I had run across back in the late '90s. (See diagram on following page.) I have been using it and teaching it regularly ever since.

I call it "Leaning into Healthy Conflict," and I chose the words "leaning in" because I believe disagreements and difficult discussions are great opportunities to build stronger relationships, and this makes it worthwhile to lean into the conflict. I realize this is uncomfortable for most people, but so is going to the funeral of a friend's parent or comforting a friend when they've just learned that they have a dreadful disease. These are uncomfortable experiences but good for the relationship.

I use the word "healthy" because when conflict is pursued early on, it's manageable and not yet toxic. I'm convinced that top leaders who do this regularly fire many fewer people than those who try to avoid the conflict in the first place.

I'm also convinced that doing this one thing 20 percent better than we do it now would make a huge difference in our churches and our ministries, not to mention our blood pressure.

In John 17:20-23 (NIV 1984) Jesus says:

> My prayer is not for them alone. I pray also for those
> who will believe in me through their message, that all of

them may be one, Father, just as you are in me and I am in you. May they also be in us so that the world may believe that you have sent me. I have given them the glory that you gave me, that they may be one as we are one: I in them and you in me. May they be brought to complete unity to let the world know that you sent me and have loved them even as you have loved me.

The unity of which Jesus speaks depends on our willingness and ability to lean into healthy conflict so that our perceived disagreements can be handled in the light instead of lurking in the shadows of our relationships.

I invite you to learn more about Leaning into Healthy Conflict by watching and listening to a 90-minute recorded webinar at www.rca.org/healthyconflict.

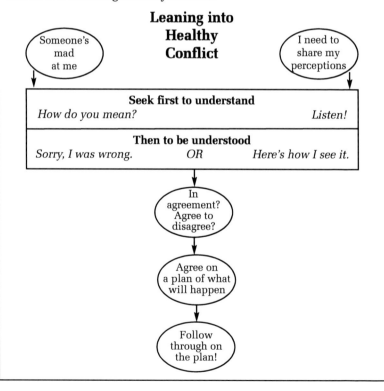

8. Rocks, Pebbles, Sand: Prioritization and Margins

On page 15 I refer to a parable about rocks, pebbles, and sand. Here's one version:

> A time-management professor was teaching a group of young emerging leaders how to manage their time effectively. He told them he wanted to make a point by demonstrating something to them. He then started to place several baseball sized rocks that were sitting on a table in front of him in a jar and asked the students to say when the jar was full.
>
> He was unable to get a sixth rock in the jar and a young man raised his hand and said, "It's full." The teacher didn't respond but instead reached under the table and grabbed a container of pebbles and put it on the table. He began to fill the empty spaces in the jar with pebbles until it was full. He looked at the students to see if someone would say it was full. They were on to him so nobody spoke up. So he reached under the table for a container of sand and commenced to fill the bits of empty space with sand. When the jar was full he looked at the students to see if they would speak. While they were tempted, no one did.
>
> He reached under the table and grabbed a pitcher of water which he promptly started pouring into the jar. When it could hold no more, he looked at the students and a young lady cautiously raised her hand and said, "It's full."
>
> The professor said, "Yes, it is. Now, what do you think the moral of the story is?"

She responded by saying, "Even when you think your life is full, you can still get more into it."

He responded, saying, "I thought you might say that, but that's not the point I want to make. The point I want you to remember as you go off and build remarkable careers and lives is this: if you don't put the big rocks in first, you'll never get them in at all."

He went on to say that the big rocks represented the most important things, the highest priorities, and the pebbles, then sand, then water were the lower priorities. He then had the students write down what was most important in their lives and their careers so they could make sure to put those things first.

I created BJ's character to be very intentional about being aware of the big rocks that needed to be in her life in order for her to be her best. She was serious and disciplined about her spiritual health, her physical health, and her emotional health.

Spiritual Health Priority

In my travels I have had pastors tell me that they basically don't have a prayer life other than the prayers they do "professionally." They report that their only Bible study is done in preparation for their Sunday worship message and not for their own edification. (Of course you can't help but be fortified by reading the Bible regardless of the motivation behind it. However, it is more powerful to also read it for personal reasons, not just to prepare for the delivery of a Sunday message.)

Too many pastors are trying to lead a spiritual organization while they themselves are spiritually dry. BJ made sure that the big rock of her spiritual health made it into her jar before the pebbles, sand, and water took over. If you are a pastor, I hope you have found the clarity and courage to make sure you stay connected to God and daily abide in Christ. If you are an elder, a deacon, or some other kind of leader in your church, I hope you will ask your pastor how he or she is doing with this and affirm the time they protect in their schedule in order to put this most important rock in their jar.

Emotional Health Priority

Another big rock has to do with a pastor's emotional health. Many pastors feel like they have nobody with whom to share their deepest concerns, anxieties, and dreams. It's not healthy to put all of the responsibility for this on a pastor's spouse. It can become toxic in their relationship, so many pastors just keep these thoughts and feelings locked up inside. No wonder burnout and other mental health issues affect so many of our pastors, and at a higher rate than most other professionals.

BJ made sure to take her concerns and anxieties to another person. She was very blessed to have her mother, Johanna, and she also gained access to a coach and several other pastors in her pastors network. In the Reformed Church in America we have spent a lot of time and money (thanks largely to the vision and generosity of Lilly Endowment, Inc.) promoting a movement to get RCA pastors into networks. We also offer them trained coaches in monthly one-on-one coaching sessions to help them gain greater clarity and courage.

We have come to believe that for the sake of their mental and emotional health all pastors should be part of a small group of pastors that will commit to support each other, hold each other accountable, and be intentional about learning together in transformational ways.

We also have a vision that any RCA pastor who wants a Christian coach will have easy access to one at little or no cost. We have made great progress toward both of these ends and yet still have a long way to go. One of my prayers is that when people read *Grace in the Heights* it will help create more momentum for pastors networks and coaching.

Physical Health Priority

Many pastors, like most people in our culture, are on a dangerous trajectory with regard to their physical health. Most pastors work too many hours, do much of that work sitting down, and eat too much unhealthy food at too many meetings. No wonder so many pastors suffer from health issues.

In my experience pastors seldom receive encouragement from someone in their flock regarding their physical well being. I don't mean periodic snide remarks about his belly or her hips; I mean real love and concern for how they are treating themselves. Many pastors are so bent on helping others that they ignore their own needs.

Did you know that over the past fifty years being a pastor has gone from being one of the safest and healthiest jobs to being one of the riskiest health-wise?

If you're a pastor, it's possible that you read about BJ's life and thought, *Of course she has time to run and study and pray; she's single and apparently doesn't have to deal with all of the urgent things I do.* I suppose this could be true. But I also created BJ to be the kind of leader who makes room in her life for the most important things, even if this might cause friction in terms of the expectations others have of her.

So if you are one of the pastors out there who is way too busy because someone's expectations are higher than what you can sustainably meet, please pardon me for not making BJ's work schedule as frantic as yours. However, I still implore you to find a way to put the big rocks in your jar!

On the other hand, if you are a lay person in your church, I ask you to consider encouraging your pastor to make time and space in his or her life to put the big rocks in the jar first. You might be surprised by the impact a little thoughtful encouragement can have in a pastor's life!

If you would like to take a deeper look at prioritizing the things you need to be effective in your life, I invite you to watch and listen to a recorded webinar called *Margins and Impact* at www.rca.org/margins.

And Finally

Thank you for reading our fable. Both Ann Saigeon and I pray that God uses it to stir you in fruitful ways on your own journey. And we ask God to bless you as you continue to grow as a Christian leader!

Rodger Price